Pe

Thomas Leitch

TV MILESTONES SERIES

Wayne State University Press   Detroit

© 2005 by Wayne State University Press,
Detroit, Michigan 48201. All rights are reserved.
No part of this book may be reproduced without formal permission.
Manufactured in the United States of America.
09 08 07 06 05   5 4 3 2 1

Library of Congress Cataloging-in-Publication Data

Leitch, Thomas M.
Perry Mason / Thomas Leitch.
p. cm. — (TV milestones)
Filmography and videography:
Includes bibliographical references and index.
ISBN 0-8143-3121-1 (pbk. : alk. paper)
1. Perry Mason (Television program) I. Title. II. Contemporary approaches to film and
television series. TV milestones.

PN1992.77.P4L45 2005
791.45'72—dc22
2005015538

∞ The paper used in this publication meets the minimum requirements of the
American National Standard for Information Sciences—Permanence of Paper for
Printed Library Materials, ANSI Z39.48-1984.

Perry Mason

TV Milestones

Series Editors

Barry Keith Grant
Brock University

Jeanette Sloniowski
Brock University

TV Milestones is part of the Contemporary Approaches to Film and Television Series

A complete listing of the books in this series can be found online at *http://wsupress.wayne.edu*

General Editor

Barry Keith Grant
Brock University

Advisory Editors

Patricia B. Erens
School of the Art Institute
  of Chicago

Robert J. Burgoyne
Wayne State University

Lucy Fischer
University of Pittsburgh

Tom Gunning
University of Chicago

Peter Lehman
Arizona State University

Anna McCarthy
New York University

Caren J. Deming
University of Arizona

Peter X. Feng
University of Delaware

To Bruce Berger
in honor of forty years of friendship

CONTENTS

America's Lawyer

Attorneys-at-law have played a prominent role in television ever since the debut of *Cross Question* in 1949. *The Black Robe, Famous Jury Trials, The Public Defender, Justice, Willy, The Verdict Is Yours, Day in Court, Harrigan & Son, The Law and Mr. Jones, The Defenders, The Trials of O'Brien, Judd for the Defense, The Lawyers, The Young Lawyers, Storefront Lawyers, Owen Marshall, Counselor at Law, Petrocelli, L.A. Law, Matlock, Night Court, Foley Square, Ally McBeal, The Practice, Boston Legal*—the list goes on and on. But when Turner Broadcasting System (TBS) ran a weeklong series in 1992 titled "Legal Weapon," there could be no doubt whose career was under review. As the unforgettable opening theme music by Fred Steiner began, TBS commenced its weeklong retrospective of *Perry Mason* reruns including fourteen one-hour segments, from "The Case of the Restless Redhead," the series' 1957 CBS debut, to "The Case of the Final Fade-Out," its closing episode nine years and 271 episodes later. Viewers who had been brought up on *Perry Mason* or had developed an addiction to syndicated reruns of the program on TBS or Court TV could spend a glorious week catching up with the unstoppable Los Angeles attorney played by Raymond Burr and his supporting ensemble: his demure secretary Della Street (Barbara Hale, who returned to introduce each TBS segment), his boyish private investigator Paul Drake (William Hopper), luckless District Attorney Hamilton Burger (William Talman), and LAPD Homicide Lt. Arthur Tragg (Ray Collins). Added to the mix were four of the twenty-six two-hour telefilms,[1] beginning with "Perry Mason Returns," that had brought the redoubtable attorney—still played by Raymond Burr, whose seventy-fifth birthday TBS was celebrating—back to a devoted public in 1985.

A Mason family reunion (William Talman, William Hopper, Barbara Hale, Raymond Burr).

Bolstered by stratospheric ratings for more than half of its nine-year run, *Perry Mason* enjoyed the longest tenure of any legal television drama. It was nominated for an Emmy for Best Dramatic Series with Continuing Characters during its first season in 1958. Raymond Burr and Barbara Hale won Emmys for Best Actor and Best Supporting Actress in 1959, a year William Hopper was also nominated. Hale was nominated again in 1961 and Burr twice more, in 1960 and 1961, when he won his second Emmy. In a 1975 poll of viewers working in or associated with the television industry, *Perry Mason* was named the favorite television series of all time.[2] Beyond these honors, which were by no means unusual for such a long-running series, the program became a showcase for what the TBS retrospective called "America's lawyer."

The epithet is both obvious and provocative. Of course Perry Mason is America's lawyer. After fifty years of television lawyers and over a century of fictional lawyer-sleuths, Mason's preeminence in his field is unquestioned. No single fictional hero has come to define a profession more completely. It is as if TBS had decided that America's doctor was Ben Casey, or Marcus Welby, M.D., or any of a dozen other contenders. Perry Mason, by contrast, has no serious rivals. Even in a world that has made celebrities of such real-life attorneys as F. Lee Bailey, Alan Dershowitz, and Johnnie Cochran, he is still America's lawyer.

The most fundamental question about *Perry Mason* is why the series and its hero achieved such enduring and iconic renown. If adaptations of Erle Stanley Gardner's best-selling novels had been so indifferently successful in feature films and radio, why did the series become so successful on television?

The most obvious reason for *Perry Mason*'s prodigious popularity is the program's most frequently noted feature: its dependence on a dramatic formula that varied remarkably little over its television life. Every episode began with a troubled family or quasi-family group, an innocent threatened with expulsion from the domestic circle or worse, and a murder for which the innocent was invariably arrested. Each accused suspect retained Mason, whose wily legal strategies in and out of the courtroom unfailingly won the client's release, most often after wringing a confession from some witness who withered under Mason's relentless cross-examination. Each segment, in short, celebrated the power of the heroic defense attorney to overcome the threats of violence and injustice. So irresistible was this power that the series shaped a generation's perception of not only fictional lawyers but, for better or worse, lawyers and the law in general.

The program was not without its necessary changes. William Talman was fired from the show in March 1960 after being charged for "gamboling without garments" at a Hollywood party.[3] (Acquitted of all charges, Talman returned to the show in December 1960, though his participation was never again equally constant.) Ray Collins was more definitively sidelined midway through the show's seventh season by illness and then death on 12 July 1964. He was replaced first by Wesley Lau, as Lt. Andy Anderson,[4] during the eighth season, and then by Richard Anderson, as Lt. Steve Drumm, in the program's ninth and final season. And of course Barbara Hale's hairstyles changed along with Mason's office decor and the Cadillacs the series regulars drove to reflect the advancing years. In general, however, the series format stoutly resisted change.

A good deal of the credit for *Perry Mason*'s success must surely go to its star. There had been movie and radio Masons before the saturnine Burr, and other television Masons would follow, most notoriously Monte Markham in *The New Perry Mason*, which was canceled midway through its first season (1973–74). None of them, however, came close to the success of the burly Canadian actor. Other great franchise heroes from Sherlock Holmes to James Bond had flourished in many different incarnations. But *Perry Mason* needed Burr, even though Burr did not need Mason, as he showed when his next series, *Ironside*, earned him six Emmy nominations and two Golden Globe nominations over its almost equally long life of eight seasons (1967–75) on NBC. Yet Burr, despite his extensive experience in movies before Perry Mason, had never before been anyone's idea of a distinguished actor or a major star. His version of Mason completely defined a hero who, except for six modestly successful films in the 1930s, a 1947 comic book, and a comic strip that ran from 1951 to 1952, had been faceless since Gardner first created him.

The triumph of *Perry Mason* is a triumph of formula—a formula that includes not only the unchanging furniture of the series' courtroom climaxes and the structure of the domestic intrigues that lead up to them but its star's iconic performance as well. Burr's purposefully limited acting fit the tightly scripted formula of his alliterative cases so seamlessly that he soon became identified as the creator of *Perry Mason*. Although Burr never contributed ideas, stories, or dialogue to the series, his identification as America's lawyer stole the limelight from the collaborators who did: a succession of anonymous writers, directors, and producers. Standing behind them all was Erle Stanley Gardner, the scrappy and resourceful California attorney who, having created Mason largely in his own image in 1933, had pioneered the television franchise and was determined to rule it with an iron fist. Nonetheless, Gardner's formative role in its creation and maintenance was gradually eclipsed by the star's incarnation of America's lawyer. What began as a case of prime-time auteurism turned into a star vehicle as the values set forth by Gardner, who had taken every precaution to ensure that he would retain creative control of the television series, were overtaken by the similar but subtly different values represented by Burr.

This book seeks to explore first the basis of a fictional formula at once enormously influential and dependent for its success on a single star and second the ways the formula fits into the broader contexts of popular fiction, mass entertainment, and American legal culture. *Perry Mason* is a television milestone not merely because it led to films like *To*

Kill a Mockingbird (1962) and television programs like *The Practice* (ABC, 1997–2004) but also because it shaped a generation of Americans' attitude toward the law. Successive chapters of this book will explore the ingredients of the program's formula, the attitude toward the law projected by that formula, the crucial migration of the program's authorial function from its creator to its star, and its subtly transformed impact when it returned to television nearly thirty years after its debut.[5] But its first order of business will be to examine the prehistory of the program—the contexts in formula fiction, literary genre and subgenre, its creator's related works, and the politics of television production in the mid-1950s that helped define its distinctive formula and laid the groundwork for its success.

Pretrial Motions

The fundamental question about *Perry Mason*—how could its formula hold sway over the popular imagination for so long?—is the one at the heart of all formula fiction and can be answered simply: the fictional genres most likely to appeal longest to popular taste are the most formulaic. In "Creative Writers and Day-Dreaming," Sigmund Freud contends more specifically that the most popular genres are those that celebrate the triumphs of "His Majesty the Ego"[1] in the guise of a hero who triumphs over impossible obstacles. John G. Cawelti proposes an equally important rule: "Formulas enable the reader to explore in fantasy the boundary between the permitted and the forbidden and to experience in a carefully controlled way the possibility of stepping across this boundary."[2] Indeed, the most formulaic genres can accommodate the most threatening material precisely because their formulas are so predictably reassuring that audiences know they can expect, if not a happy ending, at least a catastrophe that will suit the particular tastes that drove them to a given formula.

The detective story, the generic matrix of *Perry Mason*, occupies a special position in the pantheon of fictional formulas because it deals with the ultimate terrors of violent death and mystery that challenges rational explanations even as it rules out any supernatural recourse. It is difficult enough to contemplate the eventuality of our own death, but the possibility that death is radically discontinuous with life—that we could die suddenly and mysteriously under circumstances with no apparent relation to the meaning of our lives—is especially intolerable. The detective story, which seeks to discover rational explanations for the deepest mysteries of life, violence, death, and chaos, is fueled by a dialectic of order-in-disorder predicated on the central requirement of an ending that is both surprising and obligatory. It is no accident that the first certified superstar of detective fiction was the heroically brainy Sherlock Holmes or that the genre's formula achieved even more widespread popularity in England after World War I. After a generation of British youth had been killed in the trenches, it was only natural that their survivors would seek entertainment that presented violent death and baffling mystery but promised the triumph of reason and justice. Despite their potentially sanguinary subject matter, the detective stories of the English writers Agatha Christie, Dorothy L. Sayers, and Margery Allingham, the New Zealander Ngaio Marsh, and the Anglo-American John Dickson Carr were widely branded escapist fare for the civilized.[3] The domestic subgenre they inaugurated depends on a closed universe, typically centering on a cozy village or country house in which all the suspects know each other, murder is statistically uncommon, civility is observed among the survivors, and clues are fairly distributed. The result is an equally civilized competition between the detective and the reader.

Although American writers like S. S. Van Dine and Ellery Queen adapted this model to an equally cozy-seeming New York, another model emerged in America around the same time. This considerably more hardboiled model was produced for mass-circulation magazines like *Black Mask* whose low-cost paper, with a higher content of wood pulp than more aristocratic "slick" magazines like *Collier's*, spawned the term "pulp fiction." In the work of such *Black Mask* writers as Dashiell Hammett, Carroll John Daly, and Raymond Chandler, violent action, not polite conversation, was the engine of the plot and the vehicle by which the detective made his discoveries—*his*, for pulp heroes were overwhelmingly male. Indeed, their masculinity was constantly an issue in adventures that repeatedly drove them to prove their manhood. Dealing with a world that seemed more realistically violent and chaotic, such writers required a stronger dose of ritual to ballast their adventures. They found it in the conventions of stock heroes and dames and villains, tough talk, and rapid-fire battles with or without gunfire. The pulp hero was a stronger presence than the retiring heroes of Christie and Allingham because his wisecracking dialogue was more flavorful and because he was a more prominent character in the story. The hardboiled dick provided an anchor whose insouciant voice and competence in battle provided the same reassurance of ultimate order as the polished manners of Hercule Poirot or Lord Peter Wimsey.

The subgenre of stories with a continuing lawyer hero, a subgenre virtually created by Erle Stanley Gardner, holds a special and problematical place within and somewhat outside the dialectic of cozy and hardboiled detective fiction. Even though attorneys had played prominent supporting roles in detective novels from Anna Katherine Green's pioneering *The Leavenworth Case* (1878) to Frances Noyes Hart's *The Bellamy Trial* (1927), no earlier author had created the continuing character of a sleuthing attorney. The only two continuing attorneys in earlier fiction are notable in very different ways. Ephraim Tutt, the attorney created by Arthur Train for a series of *Saturday Evening Post* stories collected in *Tutt and Mr. Tutt* (1920) and other volumes, is an avuncular figure who functions less often as a detective than as a source of populist wisdom. Closer to the bone is Mason's namesake, the unscrupulous attorney Randolph Mason, created by Melville Davisson Post. In the two volumes of stories that introduced him (*The Strange Schemes of Randolph Mason* [1896]; *The Man of Last Resort* [1897]), Post set Mason the challenge of defending clients guilty of fraud, embezzlement, or even homicide. In the first and most celebrated of these stories, "The Corpus Delicti," Mason secures an acquittal for a client who has all but confessed to a murder Mason had suggested he commit. Mason argues in court that in the absence of the corpse the client had the foresight to destroy, there is no evidence that a crime was ever committed.[4] The strikingly postmodern view of the law he articulates to another client is that it has no transcendental authority but is entirely contingent, since "the word moral is a pure metaphysical symbol, possessing no more intrinsic virtue than a radical sign."[5]

Like Perry Mason's other fictional forbears, Randolph Mason serves as an advocate rather than as a detective whose primary job is to argue facts rather than uncover them. The predominant tendencies in legal fiction before Gardner had been to emphasize courtroom outsiders rather than insiders (in *The Leavenworth Case* and *The Bellamy Trial*), to emphasize the moral dilemmas dramatized by the attorney's conflicting roles as advocate and seeker of truth (in the film *Counsellor at Law* [1933] and such later films as *The Paradine Case* [1947], *The Verdict* [1982], and *Presumed Innocent* [1990]), or to explore the dramatic possibilities of loopholes in the legal system (as in the Randolph Mason stories).

Perry Mason draws in different ways on all three subgenres: the cozy whodunit, the hardboiled tale of action, and the tale of lawyers probing contradictions and loopholes in the law. It is hardly surprising that his debt to hardboiled pulp fiction is most immediately obvious, for Gardner's own earlier fiction, the work of a California attorney well known in professional circles for his ingenious tactics on behalf of his clients,[6] had been decidedly hardboiled. Beginning in 1921, Gardner published a dizzying number of short stories in a wide variety of action genres for pulps like *Breezy Stories, Top Notch, Fighting Romances, Ace High*, and of course *Black Mask*. Ruth Moore records over four hundred articles, stories, and novelettes featuring such heroes as adventurer/juggler Bob Larkin, Ed Jenkins, the Phantom Crook, and Speed Dash, the Human Fly, before Perry Mason debuted in his first novel, *The Case of the Velvet Claws*, in 1933.[7] Whatever their genre or profession, these heroes were all men of action, rarely described in more than a telling epithet or two, whose self-appointed mission was to overcome impossible obstacles en route to an unexpected but eminently predictable conclusion.

11

The Perry Mason novels freely borrow features of this formula while tailoring it to the legal profession. Gardner's hero is not only as fast-talking as any hardboiled hero; he is an officer of the court with an institutional responsibility to the laws of the land. And, swiftly as his stories move, he is not a man of action but an active thinker. Mason's habits are relatively sedentary, but his thoughts about detection, tactics, and legal strategy constantly take the most active form his world allows. Like Nero Wolfe and Archie Goodwin, Rex Stout's contemporaneous pairing of the sedentary, larger-than-life detective and a wisecracking, information-gathering sidekick clearly born on the other side of the Atlantic, Mason carries from the beginning the potential to combine cozy and hardboiled strains. Gardner's early Mason novels, like his *Black Mask* stories about his more raffish heroes, are unabashedly hardboiled in their tactics, their dialogue, and especially their pace.

As the series continues, Mason's whodunit plots are complemented by several other cozy elements. Gradually his quasi-domestic circle of regulars becomes more important than the clients who pass through the revolving door of his office. His resorts to legal finesses come to seem more obligatory than outrageous. And two rooms emerge as pivotal: the office as the staging area where Mason meets with his clients and hatches the counterplots he uses to defend them against the plots laid for them, and the courtroom as the arena in which he stages these counterplots before a participant audience.

More important in the end than either the hardboiled or the cozy formula to the Perry Mason novels is the debate over the nature of the law first developed in Post's Randolph Mason stories. Randolph Mason's own existential, purely tactical view of the law is diametrically opposed to that of both the cozy whodunit and even the hardboiled pulp mystery, in which might really does end by making right. But this severely tactical view has a decisive impact on Gardner and, through him, on all later legal fiction. Perry Mason does not accept his namesake's assumption that the law is nothing but a series of arbitrary rules that define a game between two players. But he does believe that, given a legal system that is stacked against his clients, every possible legal loophole is fair game. He accordingly has no compunction about lying to the authorities, concealing evidence, creating misleading evidence, urging his clients to hide from the police and from him, or executing courtroom maneuvers designed to outflank the district attorney on narrowly legal grounds.

The Perry Mason novels, though universally remembered as detective stories, are mostly indifferent as whodunits. With rare exceptions, their solutions turn on a single unremarkable discrepancy or hidden motive. But they shine as textbooks of legal, quasi-legal, and barely legal strategy. While never stooping to the tactics of Post's unscrupulous hero, Mason is fearless in defense of his clients' rights. His cases therefore add to the detective story's task of reconciling violent death with a rational universe a second task: to reconcile a view of the law as contingent and purely tactical with a view of the law as morally authoritative.

The cultural work of reconciling these two views of the law, which is Gardner's distinctive contribution to the mystery genre, had never arisen in his earlier fiction. Once Gardner discovered it, however, he never looked back. The torrent of stories he had poured into the pulps slowed to a trickle by the end of the decade, replaced by a steady flow of articles and books about Mason and two other continuing series. One of these, beginning with *The D.A. Calls It Murder* (1937), starred small-town District Attorney Doug Selby, a counterpart to Mason equally constrained by his respect for the law and the truth. The second, beginning with *The Bigger They Come* (1939), marked Gardner's attempt, under the pseudonym A. A. Fair, to escape from the confines of magazine fiction he thought had been trammeling the Mason franchise. Eager for the lucrative contracts magazine serialization could bring, Gardner had aimed as early as 1934 to capture this market for Mason. Chafing at the resulting need to "tone down some of Perry Mason's so-called 'unscrupulous and unethical tactics,'" he promised that "someday, after the magazines and the motion pictures get done with him . . . he can come out for one book with hypocrisy thrown to the winds and be just a damn good criminal attorney."[8] Unlike the more hardboiled new franchise, which starred flamboyantly vulgar private investigator Bertha Cool and her bantamweight operative Donald Lam in an even closer parallel to Nero Wolfe and Archie Goodwin, Mason remained eternally condemned to juggle two conceptions of the law expressing the imperatives of two different markets.

This juggling act was the engine that drove all eighty-two Perry Mason novels. Based on what Alva Johnston has aptly called "a formula within a formula,"[9] they eschew physical descriptions of people and their homes, natural landscapes, and the weather. Gardner's strengths are readily described in the negative terms made popular by Elmore Leonard's oft-quoted advice to aspiring writers: "Try to leave out the part that readers tend to skip."[10] Gardner routinely denigrated his own writing to interviewers, and it is easy to see why. He has none of Christie's talent for devising puzzles, Queen's for planting clues, Carr's for explaining away the impossible, Sayers's or Allingham's for evoking a memorable milieu, Hammett's for creating a distinctive prose style, or Chandler's for using crime as a powerful metaphor for social corruption. Yet his writing has strengths that are more essential than any of these. As he acutely remarked, "I don't consider myself a very good writer. I do consider myself a good plotter."[11] Gardner is a good plotter in the Aristotelian sense that he can unfold a story with swift and compelling logic from the opening scene.

Unlike Chandler, whose opening gambits are notable for the deceptive banality that contrasts with the quicksand of intrigue beneath, Gardner invariably presents Mason with high-concept problems that grab readers from the beginning. Why would someone steal a man's glass eye and leave an inferior counterfeit in its place? Why would a wealthy heiress take out an advertisement in a disreputable magazine looking for love? How and why would a sunbather be robbed so completely that she was left naked in the bushes of a local golf course? Once he has introduced these teasing problems, Gardner develops them with an unobtrusive gift for exposition, introducing new characters and subplots with an offhand mastery that keeps the story moving without any need for reflection or summary. The medium for this development is swift, purposive dialogue that describes problems, emphasizes conflicts, and renders any direct representation of the characters' thoughts unnecessary.

Gardner could dispense with the first-person narrative of Hammett's anonymous Continental Op and Chandler's more florid Philip Marlowe. Nor did he require the services the attentive if dim amanuensis Dr. Watson provided to Sherlock Holmes because Mason had no unexpressed thoughts. There was nothing he could not tell his clients, his private secretary Della Street, his frequent consultant Paul Drake, or a long series of police officers and district attorneys beginning with Sergeant Holcomb and Claude Drumm. Unlike the silences of Sherlock Holmes or Father Brown, Mason's silences are never pregnant; they are merely pauses for breath before the next round of legal intrigue.

However successful it was on the printed page, Gardner's distinctive synthesis of elements from the hard-boiled, cozy, and lawyer subgenres stubbornly resisted adaptation to other media. His remarks about his creation of Bertha Cool indicate his frustration not only with magazines like *Liberty* and the *Saturday Evening Post*, whose editors wanted a hero with fewer rough edges, but with Hollywood. Here the reasons for Gardner's discontent were quite different. Though he had reservations about the way it inflated Mason's professional reputation, he rather approved of Warner Bros.' film adaptation of *The Case of the Howling Dog* (1934). The success that same year of MGM's rollicking film version of Dashiell Hammett's *The Thin Man*, however, tempted Gardner's studio to remake Mason in the same mold. The Mason played by Warren William is, like Hammett's Nick Charles, a high-living, fast-drinking man-about-town. Warner Bros. broke Gardner's cardinal rule for the series by having William's Mason propose to Della Street in the second film in the series, *The Case of the Curious Bride* (1935), and showing them married in the fourth, *The Case of the Velvet Claws* (1936). Then the studio added insult to injury by writing Mason out of its adaptation of *The Case of the Dangerous Dowager* and releasing the result as a May Robson Western, *Granny Get Your Gun* (1940).[12] Furious that his damn good criminal attorney had been reduced first to one more feckless romantic hero and then to a literal nonentity, Gardner, who believed to the end of his life that "Warners proceeded to ruin Perry,"[13] vowed to have nothing more to do with Hollywood.

Mason's career on radio did not fare much better. Against the advice of his agent, Cornwell Jackson, Gardner allowed *Perry Mason* to debut on 18 October 1943 as a fifteen-minute daytime drama, a format it retained for the next twelve years. After his Hollywood experience, Gardner was so determined to retain control of the series that he wrote radio segments himself for the first three years of its run and thereafter continued to provide the original stories on which subsequent episodes were based.[14] The twelve years of the program's run are a record of virtually unbroken criticism by Gardner, who reviewed every script before the program aired but was often powerless to make the kinds of changes that would have restored more of Mason's edge. Mason, Della Street, and Paul Drake, although they were nominally the main characters, often took a back seat to characters who lingered along with their soap-opera problems for as long as three hundred episodes per story.[15] Indeed, the elements of daytime drama predominated to such an extent that after the show's final broadcast on 20 December 1955, its noncriminal elements were spun off into the television serial *The Edge of Night*.

Even before the radio program went off the air, however, a new Perry Mason was in the offing. Although the contracts Gardner was offered to renew the radio series were ever less generous, he believed that the rising medium of television could offer him not only more money but something more important that had eluded him in previous adaptations of his work to film, radio, or graphic art: creative control. He instructed Cornwell Jackson to turn down an offer to purchase the television rights to the Mason franchise outright for a million dollars. Foreseeing from Gardner's inability to write radio episodes that he would be equally unable to write a television series himself, Jackson helped him set up Paisano Productions. The corporation would "negotiate a producing arrangement and offer personalized supervision"[16] that would exert a greater measure of control than Gardner had previously achieved without committing him to day-to-day writing chores. The partnership included Gardner, several veteran secretaries who knew the series well, Jackson, and Jackson's wife, Gail Patrick, the Hollywood actress most fondly remembered for her roles in *My Man Godfrey* (1936), *Stage Door* (1937), and *My Favorite Wife* (1940). Gardner, who had wanted Patrick for the television role of Della Street, ended up with her as executive producer.

Throughout 1956 Gail Patrick Jackson sat through casting auditions. She finally decided that Della Street would be played by Barbara Hale, best known as the tireless helpmeets of *Jolson Sings Again* (1949), *The Window* (1949), and *A Lion Is in the Streets* (1953), and Paul Drake would be played by gossip columnist Hedda Hopper's son William Hopper, a relative newcomer who had played Natalie Wood's father in *Rebel Without a Cause* (1955). Sprightly, mischievous Lieutenant Tragg of homicide would be played by stage-trained Ray Collins. A veteran of Orson Welles's Mercury Players, Collins had moved from his first important Hollywood role, Boss Jim Gettys in *Citizen Kane* (1940), to such films as *The Magnificent Ambersons* (1942), *The Human Comedy* (1943), *Leave Her to Heaven* (1945), in which his attorney was considerably less active on his client's behalf than Perry Mason, and *The Racket* (1951), in which his crooked district attorney had political aspirations. Noir stalwart William Talman, who had played a doomed rookie police officer in *The Racket* but was better known as the psychopathic heavies of *Armored Car Robbery* (1950), *The City That Never Sleeps* (1953), *The Hitch-Hiker* (1953), and *Big House U.S.A.* (1955), was cast as District Attorney Hamilton Burger.

The lead role turned out to be the most difficult to cast. Fred MacMurray, William Holden, Richard Carlson, Richard Egan, Mike Connors, and Efrem Zimbalist, Jr., were all considered for the role of Mason. Eventually, however, it went to Raymond Burr, who had accepted Jackson's invitation to read for the role of Burger—for which his performance as the vindictive district attorney who sends Montgomery Clift to the electric chair in *A Place in the Sun* (1951) seemed to suit him perfectly—if he could also audition as Mason. When Jackson countered by asking him to return after he lost some weight, Burr, who struggled with weight problems all his life, lost 130 pounds. On his return he captivated Gardner, who, happening to be on the set, said, "That's Perry Mason. . . . In twenty minutes, you captured Perry Mason better than I did in twenty years."[17]

Although, like Talman, he had played heavies in most of his ninety films to date, Burr was even more closely suited to the role of Mason than to that of Burger. Like Mason, he was an intensely private man who guarded his personal life jealously. Burr shunned the spotlight, even when he was touring Korea or Vietnam to entertain American troops or raising money for the charities he supported. A compulsively conscientious performer who insisted on learning his lines by heart, he worked hard on the set, treated his fellow performers and crew members generously, and whenever he had the opportunity vanished to the northern California retreat he shared with his longtime companion Robert Benevides.[18]

By October 1956, Gail Patrick Jackson was able to shop the series on the basis of the pilot episode, "The Case of the Moth-Eaten Mink." Although NBC was the first television network to express an interest in a deal with Paisano Productions, CBS responded with a deal Gardner could not pass up: a $500,000 contract, half the net profits from the series, and complete creative control, including veto power over all scripts. By the time the program premiered at 7:30 p.m. on Saturday, 21 September 1957, the network had already banked a dozen episodes, each shot on Stage 8 at the 20th Century–Fox lot on Western Avenue, each taking from nine to eleven days to produce, each costing over $100,000.[19]

CBS seemed to be taking a chance on Mason. Lawyers had been practicing on television since 1949, with the premiere of the CBS series *Cross Question*, transformed later that year to the DuMont series *They Stand Accused*. But apart from *Willy* (CBS, 1954–55), whose small-town title character had been played by June Havoc for laughs, and *They Stand Accused* (1949–54), whose principals ad-libbed ongoing court proceedings in something like real time, their cases were restricted to actual legal files (*The Black Robe* [NBC, 1949–50]; *Famous Jury Trials* [DuMont, 1949–52]; *The Public Defender* [CBS, 1954–55]; *Justice* [NBC, 1954–56]). A heroic fictional lawyer represented a dramatic departure from earlier television attorneys.

By the middle of the decade, however, the time was ripe for the emergence of this new kind of lawyer hero. For one thing, real-life lawyers had begun to garner headlines. Thurgood Marshall had argued successfully before the Supreme Court in *Brown v. Board of Education* (1954), and plainspoken Boston attorney Joseph N. Welch had become so well known as Senator Joseph McCarthy's climactic accuser in the widely televised 1954 Army-McCarthy hearings that he was chosen to play Judge Weaver when Robert Traver's best-selling novel *Anatomy of a Murder* (1958) was filmed in 1959.

An even more promising augury for Mason's television success was the networks' move to abandon the reality-based premises of early television law series and, indeed, stand-alone dramatic programs in general. Sponsors of such venerable dramatic anthologies as *Kraft Television Theatre*

19

and *Ford Theatre* began to flex their editorial muscles in 1954, when Philco demanded to see outlines for stories to be presented on *Philco Playhouse* and pressed producers to avoid downbeat endings.[20] In response, the networks shifted their centers of production from New York to Hollywood, where they could control the product much more closely. In addition, they turned from stand-alone anthologies, whose numbers were cut in half between 1955 and 1957, to dramatic series. The new format, as Erik Barnouw has noted, "was conceived for rigid control. It invited writers to compose, to a defined formula, scripts for specified actors and often for a particular sponsor, who was inclined to think of a play as a setting for commercials."[21]

20

The timing could not have been better for the advent of a dramatic series that depended on the most tightly scripted formula in the industry. *Perry Mason* provided a model for networks that wished to shift from the writer's medium of anthology drama to the producer's (and sponsor's) medium of dramatic series. And its hero, a Los Angeles criminal attorney whose clients were always innocent, added a patina of gravitas to the network's new California image. Mason's air of incorruptibility would become equally important after the FCC scandals of 1957–58 and the quiz-show scandals of 1959, in which CBS was the only network to be indicted.[22] Despite the historically high failure rate of network programming—34 percent of all prime-time programs broadcast in 1956–57 were canceled by the end of the year[23]—CBS had every incentive to keep *Perry Mason* on the air. Their decision paid off with handsome ratings. In 1958–59, the first year in which A.C. Nielsen provided instant ratings, the series was ranked nineteenth among all prime-time programs. Its ranking improved to tenth in 1959–60, and after dipping to sixteenth in 1960–61, rose to fifth the following year before CBS removed it from its Saturday evening slot and moved it to Thursday, where it languished at twenty-third place in 1962–63.

The high casualty count during the program's debut season served as a reminder that an unvarying formula was not enough to ensure any series' survival. Even so, *Perry Mason*'s television success was surely rooted in its own formula, quite distinctive from that of Gardner's novels, whose specifics deserve a closer look.

Order in the Court

The adventures of America's lawyer follow a rigid pattern, perhaps the most rigid in the annals of television drama. By August 1961, after the program had been running for four years, the *Writer's Digest* television market list could observe, "This show has the reputation among writers as being the hardest one in Hollywood to work for."[1] From its very first episode, however, *Perry Mason* was already fine-tuning the formula that had been proposed by its pilot episode. "The Case of the Moth-Eaten Mink," first broadcast on 14 December 1957 but filmed over a year earlier, provides a fascinating laboratory for the formula, since it combines trademark elements that would become long-running features of the series with others that would be swiftly abandoned.

Among these latter roads not taken was the visual style director Ted Post established in the opening scene of the pilot episode. Post begins with a nighttime urban cityscape introducing Morey's, the restaurant where Mason and Della Street's dinner is interrupted when waitress Dixie Dayton (Kay Faylen), alarmed by a sinister man who has just entered, ducks out of the restaurant and is run down by a waiting car. Throughout this sequence and continuing later, Post, who would never again direct an episode of *Perry Mason*, establishes a noir lighting style. Even in interior shots, like the episode in Room 721 of the Keymont Hotel where Mason and Paul Drake go in response to a call for help from Morey Allen (Robert Osterloh), Post retains noir trademarks. He maintains visual interest throughout dialogue scenes by constant camera movement, cuts to new camera setups showing the same characters, and uses deep space to show Morey greeting the police in the background as Mason and Della, seated at their table in the foreground, discuss the questionable mink coat of Dixie's that Morey has left with them rather than turning it over to the police.

In retrospect, Laurence Marks and Ben Starr's adaptation of Gardner's 1952 novel is as unusual as Post's visuals. Although they do not begin, as Gardner almost always does, in Mason's office, they begin with Mason, who appears in every scene. The teleplay retains not only the leading devices that shape Gardner's plot but all of Gardner's characters, mostly under the names Gardner had given them. (Only Morey's last name is changed, from Alburg to Allen.) To compensate for this crowded canvas, however, practically no characters are developed in any detail. The regulars are given obligatory introductory scenes in lieu of any sustained development. And the characters particular to this episode are handled even more abruptly. Mae Nolan (Roxanne Arlen), the kewpie-doll waitress who comes to Mason's office to tell him that Dixie and Morey were friends before she came to work at Morey's, is given a single showy scene that leads nowhere; it is her only appearance in the episode. The episode shows no interest in the subsidiary characters as suspects because it does not focus on the question of who killed LAPD Vice Officer Robert Claremont and George Fayette, the diner whose presence had upset Dixie. Instead it asks how Mason can exonerate his clients of the charge.

As a result, the supporting characters are developed only to the extent that their testimony incriminates Dixie and Morey. Most surprising of all, Marks and Starr provide a courtroom sequence brief enough to allow the examination of only a single witness before presenting a climactic confrontation between Mason and the killer in the attorney's office—a scene that ends when the killer, brandishing a gun at Mason, is killed by Lieutenant Tragg. The scene is based loosely on an offstage scene in Gardner's novel, in which Tragg tells Mason and Della how he confronted the killer, but more closely on innumerable shootouts in contemporaneous noir features. In short, "The Case of the Moth-Eaten Mink" is written and directed very much like a noir B-feature of the period, from its stylishly dramatic opening to its violent climax.

By the time the series premiered with "The Case of the Restless Redhead" (21 September 1957), director William D. Russell had toned down most of Post's distinctive stylistic devices, as would most of the series' later directors. The arresting nighttime exterior prologue in which the terrified driver Evelyn Bagby (Whitney Blake) pulls a gun on a masked pursuer and shoots at him to frighten him off, only to reach new heights of terror when she thinks she has killed him, is in many ways a twin of the opening scene in "The Case of the Moth-Eaten Mink." Thereafter, however, the scenes are set mostly in handsome, nondescript, evenly lit interiors reminiscent of contemporaneous A-list black-and-white feature films.

The premiere episode picks up many features of the pilot that would become standard. A dramatic hook in the minute or two before the first commercial break quickly establishes the danger to the characters who will become Mason's clients, almost always before they are suspected of murder. Mason verbally spars with Tragg when they meet. Drake is identified by his signature shave-and-a-haircut

25

knock at Mason's office door and ritual greeting to Della: "Hello, beautiful." Mason relies on a distinctive habit of speech first heard in "The Case of the Moth-Eaten Mink": pausing expectantly after the first word of a sentence. "Then—they were friends?" he asks Mae Nolan of Morey and Dixie, and later asks his client, "Morey—did you kill George Fayette?"

Yet the differences are equally telling. Screenwriter Russell S. Hughes prunes both incidents and characters from Gardner's 1954 novel *The Case of the Restless Redhead*, and the remaining characters are treated predominantly as suspects for the role of the masked man who menaced Evelyn Bagby in the opening scene. Real as the danger is to the innocents Mason defends, it rarely takes the form of onscreen violence. The *to pathos*, Aristotle's term for the site of suffering, is hardly ever presented directly. Although Mason's cases always involve homicide, murders—generally limited to one per episode—are hardly ever shown onscreen and dead bodies are only briefly and tastefully displayed. The series works to transform the *to pathos* into a metaphoric site marked by verbal conflict: threats, angry outbursts, vows of revenge or punishment. The logical terminus for such conflict is a space Gardner's novels typically reserve for the climax and the series pilot downplays even further: the courtroom.

Though he spends more time in court than Gardner's Mason, the television Mason never spends more than half a given episode there, and occasionally he manages to avoid court dates entirely. Yet *Perry Mason* is appropriately described as a courtroom drama, for the courtroom establishes both procedural rules and a rigid sense of decorum for the rest of each episode. The courtroom is much more than the place to which every episode seems to be heading. It is the idealized space that best expresses the enabling paradox of the detective formula, the program's particular contribu-

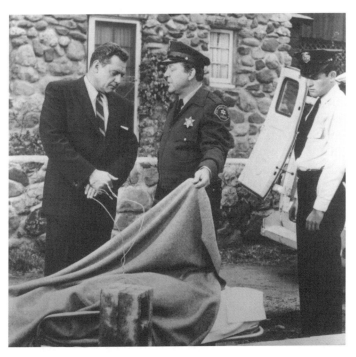

A nonviolent series' closest approach to *to pathos*: Mason looks on as a deputy (Gordon Jones) reveals the corpse of Willard Nesbitt in "The Case of the Angry Dead Man" (25 February 1961).

tion to that formula, and the social order that gives the formula such enduring appeal.

The courtroom is the most ritualized space in television. Far more than the church or the hospital operating room, it requires a precise decorum from all participants—a manner of dress and comportment, a rhetoric, a volume and tone of voice—and instantly punishes those who fail to comply. The reason might seem obvious to every citizen: the courtroom is the place where the truth about a problematic situation will be revealed under the aegis of the law. Attorneys themselves, more likely to think of the courtroom as an arena for conflict like a boxing ring, can find another reason for the precise protocol: the sharpest conflicts demand the most severe decorum in their resolution. The civility of a civil court is necessary if the attorneys for both sides are to present their clients' cases fully and fairly, since those cases will always be at odds with each other, each side's representatives politely but implicitly calling the other side's liars. In the criminal courts in which Perry Mason finds himself, the conflict is still more brutal, since the state is usually seeking to put his clients to death. The stringent rules that govern the behavior of all the participants must be as ritualistic as the rules that govern an English high tea in order to allow the brutality of the proceedings to unfold without untoward incident.

28

In Mason's case, of course, this dialectic of order-in-disorder, in which the television courtroom is at once the most orderly and the most impassioned site imaginable, is further complicated by two conventions that set Mason's adventures apart from all others. One is the defining convention of Gardner's formula: Mason will always emerge victorious from the conflict, since his clients are always innocent. The second convention also comes from Gardner. "When a client's interests are at stake, I'll do anything necessary," as Mason observes in "The Case of the Howling Dog" (11 April 1959). Since his clients are always innocent, Mason is within his rights in taking all legal means—and some that skirt the law—to secure their release by proving them innocent. This last point, a feature peculiar to *Perry Mason* that has confused two generations of viewers about the responsibilities of criminal defense attorneys, is made explicit in a rare acknowledgment Mason makes to his client, Marjorie Cluny (Lisabeth Hush), when they meet in her cell in "The Case of the Lucky Legs" (19 December 1959): "Proving you *didn't* kill [promoter Frank Patton] isn't the same as proving who *did* kill him." It is never enough for Mason to establish a reasonable doubt of his client's guilt; he must clear the client absolutely by pinning the guilt on someone else, almost always by extracting a confession.

En route to this climactic confession, Mason is willing to conceal or manufacture evidence, deceive the police about whether or not he has been present at a crime scene, sow confusion about possible murder weapons, advise his clients to hole up outside town or cross the border into Mexico, and conceal information concerning their whereabouts. Even after he gets into the courtroom, in which the truth will presumably come out, he is capable of pretending to possess evidence he does not have, bringing in charts and timetables, browbeating witnesses, asking questions District Attorney Hamilton Burger repeatedly characterizes as "incompetent, irrelevant, and immaterial," crossing lines of decorum for which he must apologize, and generally, as Burger is wont to complain, turning the courtroom into a circus.[2] His two most spectacular coups de theatre, both copied from Gardner's pages, come in this first season. In "The Case of the Crimson Kiss" (9 November 1957) he obtains a print of a suspect's lips to compare with the lipsticked print on the corpse's forehead by getting her to turn away and clapping a notebook against her mouth, and in "The Case of the Terrified Typist" (21 June 1958) he accuses his own client of murder in open court in a prefiguration of the film . . . And Justice for All twenty years later.

All these conventions, especially those peculiar to Mason's television incarnation, make the crucial point that Mason's courtroom behavior, like the place the courtroom occupies in his series, is anything but inevitable. The series could have chosen to use criminal cases to raise questions about moral problems posed by the legal system, like the contemporaneous father-and-son series The Defenders (1961–65). It could have partnered its lawyer hero with other figures from the justice system like the dogged, wisecracking police investigators in *Law & Order* (1990–) instead of making the police minor characters, the prosecutor an adversary, and the defense attorney the only continuing character who commands a strong rooting interest. And it could have followed the hardboiled conventions of Gardner's novels, the farcical Nick-and-Nora conventions of Mason's Warner Bros. movies, the soap-opera conventions of the *Perry Mason* radio series, or the noir conventions of "The Case of the Moth-Eaten Mink." By choosing to rule out all these possibilities, not just in any given episode but forever,[3] the program established the courtroom as its defining site. It is no wonder Mason's clients keep ending up in courtrooms; wherever they go, they are always on trial, and he is always in court to defend them.

30

The visual homogeneity of Mason's world begins in the courtroom, which apart from his rare excursions to the hinterlands looks the same from season to season. As the camera observes it in establishing shots from the right-hand side (typically taking the place of a jury, which rarely appears after the first season), it is a model of order. In a dark-paneled, windowless room accommodating perhaps forty people, the judge sits on a raised bench to camera right, with the witness stand to his left, closer to the camera. Burger sits on the right side of a center aisle, closer to the camera, Mason, Della, and his client on the further side. Behind them sit three rows of witnesses and spectators, who are rarely picked out by the camera, at least in the show's early years, until they are called to testify.

William D. Russell and Christian Nyby, who between them directed fourteen of the program's first fifteen episodes—the fifteenth was "The Case of the Moth-Eaten Mink"—established a camera style for these courtroom sequences that would vary remarkably little over the next nine years. Of the two directors, Nyby is consistently the more adventurous, frequently experimenting with new camera placements from over-the-shoulder shots from the gallery at the witnesses to overhead shots looking down at the witnesses. But Russell's more stolid visual style had much greater influence on the series. Long shots favor Mason's side of the courtroom (the judge's right) or, more occasionally, the witness stand seen from the gallery. Witnesses who are testifying are more often shown in medium close-up, intercut with shots of Burger or Mason examining them, reaction shots of Mason's client whispering to him or directing a stricken look at him, and, much more rarely, reaction shots from the gallery. Tight close-ups are usually reserved for Mason and the guilty party he pressures into a confession under withering cross-examination. The lighting throughout remains even and balanced, with moderate facial modeling that turns the courtroom into an unmarked, and unremarkable, space. When Mason leaves Los Angeles for backwoods Logan City in "The Case of the Drowning Duck" (12 October 1957), the courtroom naturally looks different—the walls are painted brick, and the judge's bench is so low that as he sits he is face-to-face with the standing Mason—but the visual grammar of the camera setups is exactly the same.

Following television's penchant for staging melodrama in interior spaces, the earlier sequences of each episode are shot to look like courtroom sequences. After the opening exterior long shot that begins each episode, virtually every sequence takes place indoors in a shallow, evenly illuminated space with action typically staged in a single plane and a liberal use of medium close-ups and close-ups for dialogue, which more often than not involves exactly two speakers. Of course there are exceptions to these rules over the series' long life. Mason and Della race to escape the electronically closing gates that protect the home of Wilfred Borden (George Neise) in "The Case of the Calendar Girl" (18 April 1959) before he sets his Dobermans loose. In an even closer approach to an action scene, Mason and Drake rescue ex-secretary Sally Fenner (Peggy Castle), running from the shoreline into the water from the dogs the Fenner guard has set on her in "The Case of the Negligent Nymph" (7 December 1957). "The Case of the Jaded Joker" (21 February 1959) features atmospheric coffeehouse interiors, noir-inflected lighting effects, actions frequently staged in deep space, and a track-out from a courtroom adjournment showing participants and spectators spilling out into the corridor and across the camera's path that suggests a television version of Orson Welles's *Touch of Evil* (1958). Gerd Oswald, this episode's director, is, along with Gerald Thayer, who directed the equally Wellesian "The Case of the Mythical Monkeys" (27 February 1960), the most distinctive stylist of all the program's directors. The four episodes he directed, including "The Case of the Purple Woman" (6 December 1958), "The Case of the Glittering Goldfish" (17 January 1959), and "The Case of the Lost Last Act" (21 March 1959), all show his fondness for visual invention and noir atmosphere. In general, however, visual intelligibility and homogeneity, the restriction of action to a single plane, and a transparent style that will not distract attention from the dialogue become unbroken conventions by the end of the program's second season. It is television aimed at a radio audience.

In or out of the courtroom, then, the dialogue rather than the visuals carries every scene, and Mason sets the tone and carries the greatest burden of the dialogue. The requirement for a hook that will get each episode off to a suspenseful start in the minute or two before the first commercial break means that most episodes depart from Gardner's novels, which generally begin in Mason's office. Although Mason appears in the opening scenes of a handful of television episodes, he is usually kept offscreen while conflicts develop among the episode's leading suspects. Their marital infidelities, blackmail attempts, schemes to wrestle businesses away from each other, and double-crosses inevitably lead one or the other of them to consult him, usually before a murder has been committed, always before the police have made an arrest. Mason's loyalty to his clients is therefore residual; only when he has been hired by a third party does he first meet a client who has already been arrested.

Once Mason appears, he immediately takes control, appearing in every scene for the rest of the episode and dominating them all. Indeed, once Mason has entered the story nearly every scene is shaped to give him the last word, whether or not he is in court. Even when he is curtly dismissed by Hollywood studio executive Jerry Haywood (Grant Richards) in "The Case of the Haunted Husband" (25 January 1958), he manages to tell Haywood's secretary, "Never mind, Tanner, I can find my way out." Only Lieutenant Tragg provides any real competition in his role as the commentator whose suavely menacing power is shown in his command of the last word.

Everyone remembers the program's whodunit structure. A murder is committed; circumstantial evidence, sometimes supplemented by eyewitness accounts, overwhelmingly casts suspicion on Mason's client as the culprit; and in a courtroom sequence marked by rising tension, Mason exonerates his client by extracting a confession from another suspect. Beneath this plot, however, is a much more interesting and seldom-remarked pattern that sets the relationships among the suspects against those among the continuing cast members.

Despite the magnetism that draws beautiful, alienated young women to seek Mason out as clients, virtually all of his cases revolve around a family or a quasi-family like the two roommates in "The Case of the Crimson Kiss" (9 November 1957), the zoo workers in "The Case of the Cowardly Lion" (8 April 1961), and the defense teams in "The Case of the Slandered Submarine" (14 May 1960) and

"The Case of the Angry Astronaut" (7 April 1962). In every episode, these family groups are threatened by adultery, impersonation, or greed. These threats are represented, for example, by the two young women both claiming to be the wife of Joe Bradford (Bruce Cowling) in "The Case of the Crooked Candle" (30 November 1957), the two dancers both claiming to be Lois Fenton in "The Case of the Fan-Dancer's Horse" (28 December 1957), and the two dowagers both claming to be wealthy, eccentric Amelia Corning in "The Case of the Mystified Miner" (24 February 1962). Mason's cases almost invariably have their roots in family or marital relationships poisoned by a lust for illicit sex or, more often, money. This pattern of poisoned family relationships had been established in detective fiction, from cozies like Agatha Christie's *The Mysterious Affair at Styles* (1920) to hardboiled novels like Raymond Chandler's *The Big Sleep* (1939). It had been further emphasized in television, a medium that, in John Ellis's influential formulation, "massively centres its fictional representations around the question of the family,"[4] whether the families in question are idealized (*Father Knows Best* [1954–60]), humorously dysfunctional (*All in the Family* [1971–79]), or seriously besieged (innumerable television soap operas). Atticus Finch, the ideal attorney who is also an ideal head of his family in *To Kill a Mockingbird* (novel, 1960; film, 1962), would have been right at home on network television.

Although the focus of *Perry Mason* is usually quasi-domestic, the program occasionally but revealingly indicates its ideological importance to the American way of life and even cold war politics. Air Force Captain Mike Caldwell (Simon Oakland) says in "The Case of the Misguided Missile" (6 May 1961) of the sabotage of a new missile program, "Aside from the question of patriotism and the survival of the free world, there's the millions of dollars spent on this program." His remark seamlessly links personal betrayal,

Mason and health-club instructor Veronica Temple (Leslie Parrish) in "The Case of the Left-Handed Liar" (25 November 1961): future family member or threat to family values?

financial misdealing, American idealism, and global security. Although few episodes make the stakes so explicit, each of them, by making the client's life or death depend on the verdict, makes the criminal transgressions the justice system is designed to address and potential malfunctions within the system personal and urgent.

Geopolitics and the law (I): Mason aboard the USS *Moray* in "The Case of the Slandered Submarine" (14 May 1960).

If murder is implicitly an attack on not only the murder victim but the integrity of the justice system and the American way of life, the defense against an unjust charge of murder balances the weakened or corrupted families that spawn intrigue and murder by an idealized family that works for justice. This family is represented by Mason and his legal associates. The link is made most clear-cut in "The Case of Paul Drake's Dilemma" (14 November 1959), in which Paul,

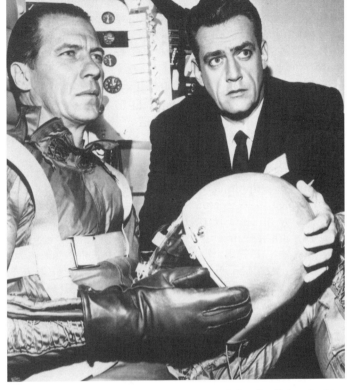

Geopolitics and the law (II): Mason with his client Mitch Heller (Robert Bray) in "The Case of the Angry Astronaut" (7 April 1962).

hired by the scheming Dameron family to funnel $25,000 in conscience money to the widow of a man Dameron's son-in-law, Frank Thatcher (Bruce Gordon), struck and killed with his car, is set up to take the fall for Thatcher's murder. After exonerating Paul, Mason tells mischief-making paterfamilias Henry Dameron (Basil Ruysdael) that he had always believed Paul's story because he was his friend. Mason contrasts their relationship pointedly with that of the Damerons: "I've never before met a person so far removed from humanity that he believed every one of his own children capable of committing a murder." By contrast, Mason's only fee, despite his earlier joke to Paul about its probable size, will be a dinner his old friend pays for.

Although Mason, Paul, and Della Street make an obvious quasi-family, it might seem odd to think of Hamilton Burger and Lieutenant Tragg as part of that family, especially since they are constantly impugning Mason's ethics. In the course of one particularly unbridled exchange in "The Case of the Haunted Husband" (25 January 1958), Tragg calls Mason "unscrupulous, conniving, unprincipled." His constant stream of exasperated criticisms, however, is complemented by Mason's respect for Burger, which never flags. The two are repeatedly shown drinking or dining together, and Mason concludes "The Case of the Purple Woman" (6 December 1958) by citing an article Burger has recently published: "A well-tried criminal case is a credit to all involved. There is no winning or losing." For his part, Burger takes every opportunity to reiterate the sentiment he voices in "The Case of the Garrulous Gambler" (17 October 1959): "The District Attorney's office is much more interested in justice than convictions." Burger and Mason are a salt-and-pepper pair fated to feud despite an enduring respect for each other and an acknowledgment that each of their jobs requires the other. It is much the same relationship on which contemporaneous husband-and-wife sitcoms like *I Love Lucy* (1951–57) and *The Honeymooners* (1955–56) were based. Tragg fits into this constellation as a charmingly menacing uncle figure whose function is taken over after Ray Collins's departure by the somewhat less charming but considerably less threatening Wesley Lau and Richard Anderson.

The quasi-domestic relationship between Mason and the other two officers of the law is economically expressed in the epilogue to "The Case of the Lame Canary" (27 June 1959).

Mason and Hamilton Burger: doubles who depend on each other for their potency.

Mason is explaining to his client, Ruth Prescott (Stacy Graham), in accordance with another of the program's unwritten rules, how he was led to suspect the real culprit by her late husband's injured canary. Burger, entering with Tragg to announce the killer's timely confession, haltingly observes that he and Ruth have already met: "I'm sure we'd both rather forget the circumstances." But he swiftly recovers from his embarrassment and goes on to deliver the episode's punch line. His bon mot—"That's the first time I've ever heard of a lame canary turning out to be a stool pigeon!"—provokes a general round of laughter that ends the series' second season by restoring the wayward prosecutor to the family unit.

The nucleus of the program's quasi-family, of course, is Mason himself. The demure good looks of Barbara Hale make her the perfect quasi-domestic counterweight to an endless series of statuesque blondes, from the private investigator Helen Bynum (Jean Tabor) in "The Case of the Dubious Bridegroom" (13 June 1959) to the three leading suspects "The Case of the Gilded Lily" (24 May 1958) groups together, whom the series routinely associate with the perils of unregulated female sexuality. If Della Street is

The rewards of regulated sexuality: Mason and Della Street share a typical moment of easy intimacy

carefully positioned to hold out the eternal promise of unconsummated romance as Mason's quasi-wife, Paul Drake, marked by his youth, breezy manner, loud sports jackets, hearty appetite for food, and ready appreciation of good-looking women, is marked as his quasi-son.

Mason's status as idealized father figure is complicated and enriched by several factors. Once he enters the courtroom, of course, he is subject to the law incarnated by a series of unsmiling, authoritarian judges. And despite occasional scenes showing him interacting paternally with children,[5] Mason never shows much fatherly warmth to anyone outside his own domestic unit. What he shows instead is a relentless appetite for conflict and a passion for the truth, the two qualities the series configures into its idealized version of the paternity best suited to mirror and correct evil or inadequate fathers like Henry Dameron. This formative paradox, which has its birth in the narrative and visual conventions of television drama and Raymond Burr's distinctive performance style as Mason, has effects that will reach far beyond the television set.

The Law According to Mason

The conventions of television drama define Mason's par-adoxical incarnation of the law by making him both unusually intimate to viewers and unusually distant from them. The best way to clarify this paradox is to consider in some detail the visual codes of a representative episode. "The Case of the Lucky Loser" (27 September 1958) begins with a twelve-shot prologue lasting just under two minutes that unfolds inside and outside a train compartment in a series of long shots (LS), full shots (FS), midshots (MS), two-shots, and medium close-ups (MCU):

Camera/Sound	Action/Dialogue
1. EXT—LS of approaching train	
2. INT—TWO-SHOT of HARRIET and LAWRENCE BALFOUR	HARRIET: I do wish I were going with you to Mexico instead of staying here in Los Angeles. LAWRENCE: Ah, this trip's going to be too dangerous, Harriet. This is the most rugged territory in the Sierra Nevada Mountains. No place

	for a woman, especially my wife.
3. MCU favoring LAWRENCE	LAWRENCE (cont.): It's almost no place for an amateur archaeologist either. Thanks for coming as far as Colegrove station.
4. MCU favoring HARRIET	She leans forward and kisses him passionately. HARRIET: Write every day, Lawrence.
5. TWO-SHOT of HARRIET and LAWRENCE	HARRIET (cont.): Don't forget. VOICE OFF: Colegrove station. HARRIET: Good-bye, my darling. (Briefer kiss.) LAWRENCE: Bye. (They go out L.)
6. EXT—Colegrove station— PAN L to arriving train	
7. CLOSER on HARRIET and LAWRENCE disembarking	LAWRENCE: Uh, better get a cab before they're all gone. (She kisses him again.)
8. LS of HARRIET crossing platform	She turns back and waves.
9. MS of LAWRENCE	He waves, then turns to re-enter train.
10. FS of HARRIET	She approaches cab, speaks with unseen driver, and gets inside. The cab drives off R.
11. MUSIC UP for LS of LAWRENCE	He disembarks again, now wearing hat, with coat over his arm, and moves off R.
12. LS and PAN R on LAWRENCE	He hurries through parking lot, gets into car, drives off R.

The opening convention of each episode, which pre-scribes domestic intrigue rather than accord, makes it likely from the beginning that at least one of the two Balfours is deceiving the other. Even though the behavior of Lawrence (Bruce Bennett) is more suspicious—why does he leave the train after pretending to go on as the background music comes up?—the visual and performative grammar of the sequence, especially shots 8 and 9, which present Harriet (Patricia Medina) as if from Lawrence's point of view but provide a much closer reverse-angle shot of Lawrence that overrides Harriet's point of view, places viewers closer to Lawrence. Although the sequence features only one shot (shot 8) that could be called a point-of-view shot, it is increasingly focalized, following a relatively neutral beginning, as Lawrence rather than Harriet experiences it, right down to the closing shot, in which he is presumably driving off to follow her. To adopt the terms television theorist John Fiske has used in another context, although "we 'see' into each, under their words, and into the relationship between them more clearly than either of them can," the "truth" of the scene lies in his experience of it, not in hers.[1]

The editing of television drama typically relies on an omniscient style that shows the audience more about the characters than they perceive about each other. In this case, Harriet's exaggerated expressions of affection and concern and Lawrence's brusque replies mark their relationship as troubled. Virtually every opening sequence of *Perry Mason* fosters an additional intimacy with one character who is anxious, suspicious, or threatened. This character usually becomes Mason's client. The opening movement of "The Case of the Lucky Loser," however, is marked by an unusually large number of shifts in intimacy from one character to another. After Lawrence follows Harriet to a hotel where she meets an unseen man, watches her leave, then enters and shoots the man, he telephones his right-hand aide, Steve Boles (Douglas Kennedy), begging for help. Lawrence's obvious distress during their phone conversation contrasts with

Boles's clipped, confident advice to keep apprehensive viewers emotionally closer to Lawrence than Boles. In the following sequence, however, a witness sees Boles dumping a corpse on a road late at night, an episode that elicits sympathy for him rather than the witness. Later, the police identify the car Boles used as that of Lawrence's nephew, Ted (Tyler MacDuff). As Harriet leads two officers up the stairs of the Balfour home to discover Ted, fully dressed, passed out on top of his bed, her evident distress marks the truth of the scene as hers. And when Ted's friend Florence Ingle (Heather Angel) consults Mason after a headline announces Ted's arrest, the camera seems to treat Florence and Mason objectively until she dodges his question about her interest in Ted, leaving viewers more closely aligned with Mason. These shifts in intimacy are not achieved through point-of-view shots but through a self-effacing grammar of acting and editing that seems to make viewers' shifts in sympathy and intimacy a natural result of the characters' behavior rather than the program's conventions of presentation.

A characteristic feature of *Perry Mason* is that once Mason is introduced in each episode, the focalization shifts exclusively to him, so that viewers experience the truth of each sequence as his truth. The pivotal scene in "The Case of the Lucky Loser" is Mason's visit to Ted's grandfather, Addison Balfour (Richard Hale), after Ted has been convicted of hit-and-run driving and given a suspended sentence. Although the sequence begins by positioning Mason to the right of a family group including Boles and Harriet, he soon crosses to the left, placing himself between the bedridden Addison and Ted. Addison charges Mason with getting the verdict overturned; Harriet tries to confirm her status as a Balfour only to be rebuffed by Addison; Boles argues that they should leave well enough alone. It is clear that these conflicts are being staged—not by the characters, but by the grammar of the scene—for Mason's benefit. His status as both the story's primary engine of action and the target audience for the other characters' big speeches is confirmed when he asks Ted what he wants, and Ted, after initially demurring, speaks passionately and almost directly into the camera in the scene's tightest close-up: "I want to know the truth. Did I do it? Was I guilty? Did I kill someone?"

This obligatory moment, in which Mason's client affirms his unquenchable desire for the truth, calls attention to Mason's most distinctive feature as a television character. He is obviously the hero of the story, with by far the greatest proportion of screen time and dialogue,[2] the most active role in the pursuit of justice, and the character whose truth is the truth of every scene in which he appears. Yet the audience is never intimate with Mason as a character. We rarely see the story from his point of view and even more rarely know what he is thinking. We have no access to his private life or, indeed, any indication that he has a private life. Paul Drake is given a healthy appetite, a series of loud sports jackets, and occasional complaints about being pulled off dates to run errands for Mason. These hints of a private life may not seem like much, but they are more than Mason ever gets. He evidently has no outside interests, no time off, no private moments, no emotional investments that are not directly connected to the practice of law. If television theorist John Corner is correct in distinguishing between soap operas, whose "imaginative centre . . . is place and people," and "series dramas," whose "imaginative centre . . . is a kind of work,"[3] then Mason represents the quintessence of series drama, a hero who is wholly defined by his job. In an important sense, he is not a character at all but simply a plot function.

This peculiar status becomes clearest when the hero moves into the courtroom. Hamilton Burger's examination of the first two witnesses against Ted Balfour are shown in a series of two-shots alternately favoring Burger and the witness paired with answering two-shots of Mason sitting silently at the defense table with Ted. The clear implication is that Burger's examinations are events staged to be watched by Mason and Ted. When Mason cross-examines Harriet, by contrast, the opening two-shot shows him in profile watching her as she sits with her face to the camera. The focus on her (but not his) performance is emphasized by a shift to a medium close-up of him asking a follow-up question and another of her answering. At this point, viewers are not simply listening in on a courtroom event but invited to play a far more active and intimate role in joining Mason in solving the mystery.

Later on in the sequence, Burger's medium close-ups invariably reveal a specific emotional reaction, usually either smug satisfaction or alarmed surprise, to developments in the case. But Mason's reveal no particular reaction. The shots do nothing to characterize him as an individual; they simply emphasize his role as agent of the plot, register of the witnesses' sworn testimony, and seeker of truth.

In this connection the program's visual grammar, which is highly typical of television drama, is complemented by Raymond Burr's distinctive performance as Mason. Burr creates the hero by maintaining an adamantine presence that admits as little emotional modulation as John Wayne in a business suit. As a result, he projects certain hallmarks of intimacy—trustworthiness, authority, power—while withholding any appeal for empathy or emotional engagement.

The leading tendency Burr emphasizes in his performance is Mason's tropism toward conflict. Listening to Burr's voice in virtually any scene of any episode reveals this tendency. Even when Mason is not in court, he cross-examines every person he meets. His most distinctive vocal inflection—letting the first word of a sentence hang in the air before continuing—carries an overtone both skeptical and hostile, and his trick of speaking faster or (more often) louder, but in exactly the same tone of voice, when he is hounding a suspect to a confession marks him as an inveterately theatrical speaker. The only way Mason has of interacting with any characters besides Della and Paul is by cross-examining them.

Not even his own clients are immune from this treatment. In "The Case of the Restless Redhead," the first episode of the program to air, Mason sets a tone that would be more prophetic than his words in this exchange with his client, Evelyn Bagby:

> Mason: Miss Bagby, you've given me trouble. . . . You didn't tell me you knew Mervyn Aldrich. . . . Did you kill Merrill?
>
> Evelyn: No!
>
> Mason: Do you know who did?
>
> Evelyn: No! . . .
>
> Mason: I suggest, Miss Bagby, that you killed him, then telephoned me and depended on your big blue eyes to convince me you were innocent.
>
> Evelyn: Maybe you'd better forget about those big blue eyes, forget about me.

The smile with which Mason greets this last response is the tip-off: He is the relentless cross-examiner whose apparent hostility can never harm the innocent on whose behalf he will fight. Mason expresses his tenderness toward his clients not by the quietness or intimacy of his manner, but by abating the sharp challenges he is compelled to make in order to test their sincerity. He is the father as lawgiver, the man who incarnates both the awful power of the law and its solicitude toward the innocent.

Burr's hooded resistance to emotional openness limited his career in movies that required him to play emotionally complex characters. But it turned out to be ideal for playing

The intimate father figure: Mason and client Betty Roberts (Joan O'Brien) examine two possible murder weapons in "The Case of the Singing Skirt" (12 March 1960).

a television hero like Mason (and later Robert Ironside), whose entire personality was subsumed by his paradoxical vocation. Although once he is introduced we experience the truth of each case as Mason's truth, we never feel any sense of his emotional truth. We are never asked to feel his anxiety, his exasperation, his doubt, or his exultation in any but a professional connection. Except in quasi-domestic scenes with Della and Paul, we never experience Mason as a private

The official father figure: Mason remains remote even as the center of attention.

individual, and the only way he has of establishing significant relationships with others is by cross-examining them. He is something both more and less than a fictional character: the iconic defender of the weak and the seeker of truth.

This description of Mason may make him sound like Sherlock Holmes, and, indeed, Mason inherits a great deal of his emotional aloofness from Holmes. But the absence of Dr. Watson marks a crucial difference between Mason and Holmes.

Mason has no confidant or amanuensis who humanizes him. He consults Della and Paul only to solicit their professional help or to ask them rhetorical questions. Instead of Dr. Watson, Mason relies on the discourse of television drama, a non-human surrogate as impersonal as himself, to maintain his heroic status while preserving his distance from the audience. If all the suspects in a given episode are intended to be suspiciously opaque until one of them is unmasked as the killer, Burr plays Mason as comfortably opaque. He is a hero with no emotional investments, no important nonprofessional relations, no private life whose lack of these humanizing attributes never becomes an issue. Unlike the suspects, who exist only to be revealed for what they are, his authoritative opacity is a guarantee that he will never be fully revealed, because there is nothing hidden to reveal.

The history of network television is largely a history of performers from Lucille Ball to Roseanne Barr whose fictional roles became conflated with their offscreen personas. Unlike feature films, television encourages close identifications with characters who pose as guests in America's living rooms week after week. The medium typically seeks to ingratiate its heroes and heroines by grafting their personalities onto the personalities of famous performers who would be welcome in any home. *Perry Mason*'s twist on this formula is to root its hero in two essentially unknowable forebears. One is Gardner's Mason, who cruised through eighty-two novels leaving scarcely a trace of any private life or even any physical evidence of his appearance. The other is Raymond Burr, whose passion for privacy was well known in Hollywood even before he took on his most famous role. Their eminently companionable unknowability, which lays the groundwork for a Mason intimate in some ways but aloof in others, becomes an indispensable foundation of America's lawyer.

Mason's other foundation, of course, is what might be called America's law—the law according to Perry Mason, familiar to millions of weekly viewers but practiced nowhere outside CBS. The requirement that television drama be dramatic demands that Mason, unlike most real-life criminal defense attorneys, spend most of his professional life in court defending clients who stand accused of murder. Once he gets there, however, Mason's experience of the law differs sharply from any experience his viewers, whether or not they are lawyers, could expect in an actual courtroom. Pop television commentator Sam Frank has observed that the program misled two decades of viewers about

> how a trial lawyer operates; how a district attorney's office functions and the extent of the head D.A.'s involvement in murder trials; the function of a preliminary hearing as opposed to that of a trial; how much time elapses before a person is charged with murder and the start of the trial; how much leeway a trial judge would give a grandstanding gimmick-prone lawyer like Mason before ruling his tactics as way out of line; the likelihood of a witness stand confession to a murder, especially when it is the result of badgering; and the ratio of wins to losses of a seasoned defense attorney and an equally seasoned prosecutor.[4]

Indeed, the National Association of County and Prosecuting Attorneys once complained that the series and its ilk were prejudicing real-life American jurors against prosecutors in favor of defense attorneys and leading them to expect courtroom confessions or equally dramatic and definitive conclusions to every case.[5] Real-life district attorney W. H. Lewis observed in a *TV Guide* article that he had never seen a defendant admit guilt in the course of a criminal trial.[6] Ten years after Raymond Burr's death, law professors across the country still exhort their students not to adopt Perry Mason as their presumptive model for legal procedures and professional ethics. Acquittals are normally secured, they point out, not by establishing the guilt of another party but by creating a reasonable doubt in the minds of the judge or jury of the defendant's guilt; by putting defendants on the witness stand to testify in their own behalf;[7] or by offering a counternarrative of the defendant's innocence more compelling than the prosecution's narrative of the defendant's guilt. The obligatory scene in which Mason, confronting a client who has just been arrested for murder, asks point blank whether or not his client committed the crime sets a perilously high standard for real-life lawyers. Any lawyer whose client responded by admitting guilt would lose a number of possible defense strategies that would now depend on suborning perjury or serving as an accessory after the fact. Certainly no lawyer whose client matched his or her candor in admitting to a crime would be able to argue, as Mason unfailingly does, the SODDI defense: Some Other Dude Did It.

Mason can make and win this argument, of course, only because his clients are invariably innocent, a luxury available to few attorneys in real-world criminal practices. The moral and technical innocence of Mason's clients is the defining feature of the franchise, one that sets it apart from such celebrated legal television series as *The Defenders* (CBS, 1961–65), *L.A. Law* (NBC, 1986–94), *Law & Order*, and *The Practice*. All of these later dramas shift their focus from the question of identifying the guilty party to either problems with the justice system and its laws or contradictions in the nature of the legal profession. *Perry Mason*'s commitment to a format in which Mason's clients were always innocent decisively ruled out the kinds of moral complications later series routinely explored.

Perry Mason's own distinctive formula depends on three assumptions about the law. The first is that innocence and guilt are categorical and absolute. Harvard law professor Arthur Miller has observed that "because the law seeks to draw a measure of harmony out of considerable discord in our society, its basic approach to any significant problem involves a compromise."⁸ People who kill someone in a motor vehicle accident, a scuffle, or a fistfight, or in defense of life or family or property are responsible for the victim's death, but the question of their guilt is rarely black and white. They may be charged with second-degree murder, manslaughter, negligent homicide, or leaving the scene of an accident, and, once charged, they may well be acquitted because guilt and innocence have no absolute status before the law. In Mason's zero-sum world, clients are either innocent or guilty (except that they are never guilty, not even of misdemeanors), and one person's innocence is a function of another's guilt.

The second assumption of the Perry Mason formula is one it shares with virtually all detective fiction: the truth shall set you free. Mason constantly exhorts his clients to level with him because it simplifies his job and protects him from unwelcome surprises in court. But it is also in their own best interest, since only the guilty need the protection of lies. Once the deceptions and frame-ups and red herrings have been cleared away, the innocence of Mason's clients is so patent that even Hamilton Burger invariably acknowledges it and indeed often cooperates in bringing it to light. Because the truth, once perceived, is both self-evident and transcendent, rival truths never battle each other in Mason's courtroom. When the truth is challenged, it is always by misunderstandings that must be cleared up or lies that must be discredited.

This transcendental status of legal truth in the Mason canon is rooted in the third and most distinctive feature of the Perry Mason formula. Each of Mason's cases is defined by a movement toward the revelation of a criminal and moral truth absolutely congruent with legal truth. If the arrest and arraignment of Mason's clients is a miscarriage of justice, their vindication marks a carriage of justice, the normal operation of the justice system from which their earlier troubles had marked a temporary swerve. In its normal operation, the system's function is to produce a legal truth—in the case of Mason's clients, a verdict of not guilty (or, more precisely, a dismissal of criminal charges *tout court*)—that corresponds exactly with moral or ontological truth. Mason's courtroom, to put it differently, is dedicated to the proposition that there is such a thing as legal truth (truth that the law reveals) as opposed to truth under the law (truth that the law creates).

Beneath this view of the law is the bedrock myth that behind the law stands the Law. Mason's clients can trust his injunctions to tell the truth for the same reason they can trust him and the justice system he represents: because the laws of that system are just. The obvious antithesis is *The Practice*, in which "the system is a largely dysfunctional institution in which justice, presented here as synonymous with morality, is to be found primarily in the interstices of the legal code."[9] Mason, by contrast, shares the faith of fundamentalist theologians that the law of the land is based on universal principles of justice that will ultimately be recognized by all participants in a legal action, even if that action is a military court-martial or an East German court that deprives Mason and his client of most of the rights they enjoy in civilian America.

This theological or transcendental view of the law is challenged in every episode of *Perry Mason* by a fundamental reality of the American legal system: the adversary nature of all court proceedings requiring the prosecution and the defense in a criminal case, like the two disputing parties in a civil suit, to present competing narratives that cannot both be credited. By identifying one of these narratives as the truth and the competing story as a misreading, a deception, or a lie, this resolution installs the criminal defense attorney as the ultimate check on the potentially calamitous power of the state. Mason, a far more consequential figure than the clients and suspects who come and go every week, battles to persuade the court that his story of the crime should carry greater weight than the story Burger offers on behalf of the people of California. Meanwhile, the viewing audience, secure in their knowledge of the program's formula, can watch each episode in the certainty that the climactic confession, in accordance with the dictates of network television, will unite legal, moral, and ontological truth in a definitive resolution unrivaled by even the most definitive-seeming actual cases.

In the world of the American legal system, based on case law and ultimately on constitutional law, the law may seem eternal, but it is always subject to change. In a culture that reveres the law but nervously acknowledges its mutability, even its susceptibility to hijacking by bad lawyers, legislators, and jurists making and enforcing bad laws, Perry Mason provides the comforting myth that the law is transcendental, immutable, and accountable to a power beyond the reach of politicians, advertisers, and mischievous citizens. The series does not identify this power with any religious or philosophical system of belief but simply implies that the truth is its own authority. *Vox populi, vox dei*, with the people represented by the entire legal community, from the judge to the defendant, a community that gives pride of place to Mason's own quasi-domestic establishment. When everyone onscreen can agree on the justice of a verdict, there is no need for philosophical justifications. By aligning the criminal law with a transcendental Law that remains as immune to critical scrutiny as Mason's private life, *Perry Mason* rescues the law from its own excesses. Instead of blighting innocent lives by forcing citizens to account for themselves, Mason's law operates in the name of a transcendental Law whose authority everyone onscreen and off can accept precisely because it is never specified.

America's lawyer, then, represents a dream of the American legal system personified by a non-American actor whose most notable preparation for the role had been ten years of playing movie criminals. At once incarnating and correcting the legal system, he can provide his clients with the kind of justice that is secured ultimately by their own behavior, however guilty it seems. The system under which he operates conflates truth with innocence and innocence with a guarantee of legal protection ultimately incorruptible by competing interests, counterclaims, or legal procedures. Mason's courtroom is what Richard Dyer might call a legal utopia, a space where "specific inadequacies in society"[10] work through the formulas and institutions of popular entertainment to generate an ideal corrective.

It is no wonder that television viewers, naturally projecting themselves as both innocent citizens and potential victims of crime rather than its perpetrators, embraced a view of the law whose idealistic absolutism was so remote from the workings of the actual American justice system. To the foundation of all popular formulas—the attempt to transmute cultural anxieties into the conflicts of mass entertainment—television networks added the encouragement to preserve and celebrate the status quo of the social institutions they explored. This tendency did not of course affect every legal series in the same way. Earlier series like *Justice* and *The Public Defender* had dramatized actual case files. Contemporary series like *The Defenders* explored ethical dilemmas posed by the vagaries of the law. More recent series like *Law & Order* and *The Practice* fictionalize cases from contemporary headlines. *Perry Mason*, more conservative than any of the others, reduced the possibility of debate over legal problems to questions of factual guilt or innocence. In doing so, the series became part of what Jürgen Habermas has called "a refeudalization of the public sphere"[11] in which rational debate among citizens holding equal power over public questions is replaced by an unequal relationship in which television networks, suppliers driven by commercial interests, provide a simulacrum of public debate designed to be uncritically accepted by passive consumers.

Communications theorists have traced this legacy of *Perry Mason* to countless crime shows and their viewers. Noting that television provides "distorted information about the legal process [that] competes with more accurate information from other sources for attention," James M. Carlson argues that "television entertainment, specifically police-crime shows, promotes social stability and control by reinforcing the perceived legitimacy of current power arrangements."[12]

Wende Vyborney Dumble draws a similar conclusion in her analysis of three more recent series featuring or based on real-life court proceedings—*The People's Court* (1981–93), *Divorce Court* (1986–90), and *Superior Court* (1986–90)— that seek to reconcile the realities of the American justice system with the imperatives of television drama. Dumble observes that all three "provide a positive message that justice is accessible and comprehensible *so long as viewers are not participants in genuine trials*. The learning that takes place is essentially passive; the result is a positive view of the justice system and a largely realistic understanding of its limitations, without any incentive to participate."[13] This diagnosis is as true of the fictional Mason's courtroom as of the real-life Judge Wapner's. By encouraging viewers to shift their sympathies from an innocent victim of the law's power to a legal avenger who can win acquittal in the most hopeless cases, *Perry Mason* fosters a fatalistic view of the law in which the hope of being represented by Mason becomes literally utopian. In Gardner's novels, this utopian tendency had been complicated by the ambivalent nature of Mason, a legal maverick willing to bend every rule in the book to get his clients off. Over the course of his nine-year television practice, this divided hero and the legal debates his tactics ignited took a very different turn.

The Case of the Overdetermined Auteur

One of the leading tenets of television studies is that "the producer [is] the auteur of the American commercial television series."[1] But it was not always so. The early 1950s, the great period of live dramatic anthology programs that produced so many masterpieces of the genre like "Marty" (1953) and "Requiem for a Heavyweight" (1956) that it has often been called television's Golden Age, was dominated by a notion of "the writer as auteur."[2] As early as 1950 screenwriters competed with novelists, whose series characters they were adapting for auteur status. Beginning with Ellery Queen that year, any number of fictional detectives, most of whom had already enjoyed active Hollywood or radio careers, made the leap to television: Martin Kane in 1951, Boston Blackie and Flash Casey in 1952, Pam and Jerry North in 1953, Sherlock Holmes in 1955, Charlie Chan, Mike Hammer, and Nick and Nora Charles in 1957. Most of these series, borrowing little more than their concepts and detective heroes from their ostensible sources, reflect crucial differences between auteurship and authorship. Alfred Hitchcock was the unquestioned auteur of *Alfred Hitchcock Presents* (1955–62) and *The Alfred Hitchcock*

Hour (1962–65), even though he wrote none of the series' scripts and directed only a small fraction of them, because he was such an inimitable host. *Zane Grey Theater* (1956–61) boasted at least two candidates for auteur: Western novelist Grey, whose novels provided material for many of the program's stories, and Dick Powell, who hosted the program (also known as *Dick Powell's Zane Grey Theater*) and occasionally starred. Although Gardner's name was absent from his own program's title, the series advertised its close connection with him every week, beginning with the episode labeled "Erle Stanley Gardner's *The Case of the Restless Redhead*."

Gardner's authorship of the series, of course, extended far beyond this gesture. Unlike Grey, who was unable to oversee his weekly series because he had died in 1939, Gardner had set up Paisano Productions specifically to maintain control of the series. Although Paisano Productions was a partnership including Gardner, three of his secretaries, Cornwell Jackson, and Gail Patrick Jackson, the no-nonsense memos he dictated establishing ground rules for Mason and the series—"Mason is clever. He is quick. He is ingenious—but he is not a smart aleck"[3]—left no doubt who its auteur would be.

Gardner's authorship of the Perry Mason novels was only the most obvious of Gardner's qualifications for the position of legal television auteur. Like his most famous creation, he had been a successful attorney whose most notable courtroom triumphs had depended on his knowledge of variously dramatic and recondite legal procedures. In 1948 he had helped establish a legal foundation dedicated to clearing wrongly accused defendants, and his book about the foundation, *The Court of Last Resort*, won the 1952 Edgar Allan Poe Award for true crime. From the beginning, however, Gardner's television auteurship was a far cry from authorship. Although his enormous Perry Mason backlog—fifty titles between 1933 and October 1956, when "The Case of the Moth-Eaten Mink" was produced—made him a natural for the role of auteur, the nature of his participation was very different from that of his participation in the *Perry Mason* radio program. Gardner never wrote or rewrote a line for the television series or took any active role in production, leaving such day-to-day tasks as auditioning writers, choosing performers, and vetting scripts to Gail Patrick Jackson.

Nor were individual episodes of the series obliged to follow the Gardner novels they adapted very closely at all. Many of the series' screenwriters felt free to reassign character traits and functions. The identity of the killer is changed in "The Case of the Green-Eyed Sister" (8 February 1958) and "The Case of the Singing Skirt" (12 March 1960). "The Case of the Lonely Heiress" (1 February 1958) presents a new victim along with a new killer, and in "The Case of the Black-Eyed Blonde" (14 June 1958), the new murderer makes essentially the same dying declaration as the original culprit after being mortally wounded in a car chase recast from Gardner's 1944 novel, which had shown Mason himself, rather than the killer, chased by a traffic cop as he sped to the denouement.

What remained generally untouched were the features that had made Gardner's long-running series such an attractive franchise. The heroic criminal attorney still defends clients who invariably turn out to be innocent. The series is marked by inventive opening situations, a mastery of unforced exposition, a swift narrative pace, an effortless presentation of figures who all have intriguing relationships to the crime without simply being parallel suspects, staccato expository dialogue between characters who eternally seem to be spoiling for an argument, ingenuity in orchestrating complex dangers, and Mason's corresponding ingenuity in devising technically legal schemes to get his guilty-looking clients off the hook.

Unlike Gardner's novels, the television series kept its cast of regulars as constant as possible. The first of the novels, *The Case of the Velvet Claws* (1933), had introduced Mason, Della Street, and investigator Paul Drake in much the same roles they would assume throughout the novels and television episodes. But Gardner did not introduce Lt. Arthur Tragg to the series until the seventeenth novel, *The Case of the Silent Partner* (1940), where he is described as the "live wire" that "they've just put . . . on Homicide."[4] And although Burger had debuted as early as the sixth novel, *The Case of the Counterfeit Eye* (1935), he did not emerge until 1950 or so as the front-runner in the pack of prosecutors with whom Mason routinely crossed swords to become a series fixture.

Even after "The Case of the Restless Redhead" established visual and dramatic conventions for the series quite distinct from the conventions of "The Case of the Moth-Eaten Mink," the series continued to change. The most obvious shift was away from adaptations of Gardner's novels to original teleplays. Although 37 of the 39 episodes in the program's first season were adaptations of Gardner novels, only 14 of the 39 episodes in the second season were adaptations. Having essentially exhausted Gardner's substantial backlist in these first two seasons, Paisano Productions was thenceforth limited in each of its seven subsequent seasons to between one and five adaptations, usually episodes based on Gardner's most recent novels or remakes of earlier adaptations.[5] The episodes based on Gardner's most recent work, though limited in their frequency by their author's inability to produce more than two or three new novels a year, offered faithful readers the bonus of appearing a year or more ahead of the novels' inexpensive paperback reprints.[6]

As the proportion of original teleplays in the mix rose, the series formula began to change. Gardner's satisfaction with the conventions he had established early on led him to resist changing anything except the elements required by new installments: new problems for Mason to solve, new casts of characters embodying the same familiar types, and new legal tactics in and out of the courtroom. More restless screenwriters unconstrained by the need for fidelity to one of his novels often sought novelty by adding new material Gardner had never considered. Apart from local novelties, the underlying formula itself was subject to more subtle transformation.

The changes original teleplays made in the formula fell into three categories. First was the showcasing of guest stars, a device obviously unavailable to Gardner the novelist. Most of the non-regulars in the series were played by journeyman television performers whose faces were more familiar than their names. Apart from the dozens of rising performers who would someday become famous,[7] the program regularly showcased such established Hollywood figures as Fay Wray, Arthur Hunnicutt, Otto Kruger, Bruce Bennett, James Coburn, Hugh Marlowe, Zasu Pitts, Dan Seymour, and singer Frankie Laine, most of them playing victims or clients. Such figures were typically given showy roles, often playing hotheaded characters who provided an effective foil for the imperturbable attorney. Their appearances aimed for maximum impact without threatening the primacy of Mason. The guest stars who did upstage Mason were those called in to replace an ailing Raymond Burr while he recuperated from a back injury during the winter of 1962–63. As Mason made a trip to Europe, conferring with his replacements via brief shots from his bedside, his place was taken by four different attorneys. In the series' most spectacular casting coup, Bette Davis played Constant Doyle in "The Case of Constant Doyle" (31 January 1963). Michael Rennie played Prof. Edward Lindley in "The Case of the Libelous Locket" (7 February 1963). Hugh O'Brian played Bruce Jason in "The Case of the Two-Faced Turnabout" (14 February

1963). And Walter Pidgeon played Sherman Hatfield in "The Case of the Surplus Suitor" (28 February 1963). Throughout these personnel changes, as J. Dennis Bounds has noted, "the episode's formula stays intact."[8]

The second novelty was the introduction of an unusual subculture. With few exceptions like *The Case of the Drowsy Mosquito* (1943), which had reflected the author's love of wide-open spaces by carrying the attorney from Los Angeles to the desert town of San Roberto, Gardner had never taken

The art of the guest star: Daphne Whilom (Zasu Pitts) looks out along with the painted figure behind her in "The Case of the Absent Artist" (17 March 1962).

Mason outside his own subculture of business deals, professional men and women, and legal problems. No matter how bizarre the problems Mason faced, he tended to pull his clients into his own tightly defined circle instead of entering into their own. The result was a pattern of personal, domestic, professional, and mercantile clashes that resisted any broader metaphorical casting as cultural conflict. This pattern changes, however, in newly scripted episodes that not only add such destinations as East Germany, San Diego,

The rare guest star who upstages Drake and Mason: the title character in "The Case of the Bashful Burro" (26 March 1960) arrives in court to testify.

Absent Mason: aided by Drake, Bette Davis takes a turn as defense counsel in "The Case of Constant Doyle" (31 January 1963).

numerous small towns in California, and several military bases, but explore subcultures closer to home. Several episodes revolve around mysterious paintings, reflecting Raymond Burr's interest in art. Unlike the television adaptation of Gardner's novel *The Case of the Ice-Cold Hands* (23 January 1964), which rapidly moves away from its opening scene at a racetrack, "The Case of the Jilted Jockey" (15 November 1958) enters more fully into the world of horse racing. "The Case of the Twice-Told Twist" (27 February 1966), the only episode filmed in color,[9] explores the world of juvenile delinquency, and "The Case of the Jaded Joker" (21 February 1959) the world of beatniks and cool (though white) jazz. Although African Americans are as rare in *Perry Mason* as in *Gunsmoke* (1955–75), Asian Americans from the Pacific Rim take their place as a less threatening, indeed threatened, racial Other. "The Case of the Blushing Pearls" (24 October 1959) is typical in its presentation of Japanese American culture as quaint, exotic, and endangered by uncouth Americans. The episode calls its heroine Mitsou Kamuri (Nobu McCarthy) a "stranger in a strange land" and takes the time to explain customs of Japanese dress and hara-kiri. In contrast to Gardner's novels, whose centripetal force pulls variations in character and setting toward a single center of legal intrigue, the original teleplays that take Mason outside his accustomed circle become more extroverted and diverse.

The most celebrated variations in the formula involve threats to the core cast. Paul Drake, framed for murder, becomes Mason's client in "The Case of Paul Drake's Dilemma" and is poisoned nearly to death when he goes undercover as "Rod Steele" in "The Case of the Carefree Coronary" (17 October 1965). Hamilton Burger pleads with Mason to take on the defense of his old friend, hunting guide Jefferson Pike (J. Pat O'Malley), in "The Case of the Prudent Prosecutor" (30 January 1960) and then sits restlessly in the gallery cheering him on sotto voce. Mason himself is briefly appointed a special prosecutor in Waring County, California, in "The Case of the Fraudulent Photo" (7 February 1959), and Burr plays a striking double role as Mason and Grimes, an old seadog hired to impersonate him in order to discredit him, in "The Case of the Dead Ringer" (17 April 1966).

The most eagerly anticipated of all variations, however, was the occasion on which America's lawyer might actually lose a case. Although Raymond Burr joked that Mason lost plenty of cases that did not happen to air on Saturday evenings, his unblemished track record made it possible to generate considerable suspense about the possibility that he might someday go down in defeat. In "The Case of the Terrified Typist" (21 June 1958), Mason's client, Duane Jefferson (Alan Marshall), faithfully following Gardner's 1956 novel, turns out to be guilty, but then, by an ingenious bit of legalistic hair-splitting, turns out not to be Mason's client after all. And "The Case of the Deadly Verdict" (3 October 1963), the most notorious episode in Mason's television career, begins in the courtroom, where Janice Barton (Julie Adams) is found guilty of murder. Although Mason files appeal after appeal, it is his activities as a detective, not a lawyer, that reverse the verdict when he urges family servant Emily Green (Joan Tompkins) to set a blackmail trap for the real criminal. The novelty of the concept was so powerful that Gail Patrick Jackson issued a publicity release a month before it ran, just as the new television season was beginning, to announce that the episode would begin with a jury finding Mason's client guilty. To this day the seldom seen segment, removed for many years from the package of reruns offered in syndication, remains the most celebrated of all Mason's televised cases.

Despite these threats, Paul Drake never died or was found guilty of murder, and Mason never lost a case. The greatest impact on the series' core formula was produced by a series of more subtle changes that departed so clearly from Gardner's concept that they installed a new auteur in his place. The need for a brief, suspenseful prologue before the first commercial meant that Mason, whose office provided the almost invariable setting for Gardner's opening scenes, was banished from all but a handful of television openings.

The ultimate tease: a Dewey-defeats-Truman headline designed for, but not used on, "The Case of the Deadly Verdict" (3 October 1963).

Although Gardner's Mason had often maneuvered so successfully on his clients' behalf that they never had to appear in court—two of his first three published cases contain no courtroom scenes—television episodes without such scenes are highly unusual.[10] A far more frequent formula, equally congenial to production economics and suspense-loving viewers, staged the entire second half of each episode in the same courtroom.[11] Developing their own more specialized formula within the formula of one-camera television drama, episodes cut with increasing rapidity between two-shots of Burger or Mason examining witnesses and close-up reaction shots of suspects watching from the gallery. The tension was broken only when Mason provoked a confession from the witness he was examining—or, in an even bolder stroke, from a witness in the gallery who had disintegrated under the pressure Mason was applying elsewhere.

This endlessly parodied handling of the courtroom formula owes less to Gardner's novels than to emerging practices in such diverse contemporaneous television crime dramas as *The Naked City* (1958–63) and *77 Sunset Strip* (1958–64). Although the rapid-fire back-and-forth of Gardner's cross-examinations makes his courtroom scenes memorable, it is rare that they make up even a third of a given novel. The unmotivated reaction shots of suspects in the gallery who look increasingly guilty as the camera returns to them are, of course, a peculiarly idiomatic feature of television that have no counterpart in Gardner.[12] Neither do the confessions Mason forces in court, at least not before 1958. Indeed Gardner's Mason is generally content to explain his knowledge of the crime to Della Street and Paul Drake or to the district attorney's office instead of confronting the murderer directly.

That may well be because the Mason of Gardner's novels typically defines his job as making the best possible case for his client rather than accusing and breaking down the actual culprit in court. In his professional role as a sleuthing lawyer, Mason bears less resemblance to earlier fictional sleuths like Sherlock Holmes than to his namesake Randolph Mason, and for that matter to the legion of hard-boiled heroes Gardner had already invented before Mason. Gardner's leading contribution to detective-story history had been to root an action hero in the courtroom, whose formulaic conventions make even the smallest departure from decorum a dramatic event.

Gardner had conceived Mason as a hardboiled hero who could use quasi-legal maneuvers and canny cross-examination as more politic substitutes for fisticuffs and gunplay. In his early novels, Mason is not above breaking and entering, tampering with evidence, and risking contempt citations in the service of his clients. Even before his first television close-up, however, Mason's legal chicanery had been toned down to win lucrative prepublication offers from slick magazines like the *Saturday Evening Post*, which serialized one or two of Gardner's novels annually from 1953 through 1962. Television completed Mason's transformation from a hired gun with a law degree to a principled seeker of truth and justice. "The Case of the Lucky Loser" (27 September 1958) purges Burger's accusation in Gardner's novel that Mason has actionably withheld fingerprint evidence that would have incriminated his client. "The Case of the Howling Dog" (11 April 1959) whitewashes Mason's client, Evelyn Forbes (Ann Rutherford, playing the character named Bessie Forbes in Gardner's novel and Bessie Foley in the film adaptation), by eliminating the suggestion that had ended both Gardner's novel and its Warner Bros. feature adaptation that Bessie might have killed her ex-husband in self-defense. And the television Mason never loses an opportunity to exhort his clients to tell him not only the truth but "the *whole* truth," as he tells Jefferson Pike in exasperation in "The Case of the Prudent Prosecutor."

In "The Case of the Angry Mourner" (2 November 1957), Mason tells his client's mother, Belle Adrian (Sylvia Field), when she first approaches him on his vacation that "what you need is a detective. I'm a lawyer. I do employ a good agency, however." This is too modest. Mason combines both roles in ways whose contradictions the series takes pains to downplay. As Mason's remark suggests, his series apparently reserves the role of detective to Drake, leaving Mason free to practice the law. But Drake finds only what Mason directs him to look for. He never has any hunches of his own or any theories about the case; he is merely a gatherer of facts. It is Mason who carries the detective's traditional burden of thinking.

Mason the detective vindicates his clients not by developing a legal strategy that will ensure a courtroom triumph but by establishing conclusive evidence of another party's guilt. Hence Mason the lawyer conflates not only the roles of tireless advocate and officer of the court but the roles of defender of the innocent and scourge of the guilty. Instead of using the law against the law, the television Mason valorizes the legal system by incarnating its guarantee of protection to the innocent. In Gardner's novels, the law and the facts repeatedly happen to coincide; in the television series, Mason repeatedly professes his faith that they must coincide. The result shifts from Gardner's exploration of a canny defense lawyer's arsenal of tricks to a triumphalist anatomy of the law's authority. The television series casts Hamilton Burger as the legal bogeyman and Mason as the legal champion who personifies everything that is good, true, and just in the law. By vindicating his clients week after week, Mason ultimately vindicates the legal system itself, incarnating the irresistibly appealing myth that moral justice, truth, and the law are congruent. As Gardner's wily Mason yielded to television's avuncular Mason, his brand of authority shifted accordingly from the deviser of clever tactics to the incarnation of an equivocal authority that cross-examines everyone, even his own clients, before ultimately pronouncing them innocent.

Given this realignment, it is hardly surprising that Gardner's position as the program's auteur is ultimately superseded by a more palpably heroic figure. Gardner continued to review every weekly script, though primary responsibility for maintaining the series formula gradually passed to lawyer-producer Ben Brady, lawyer-author Gene Wang, the series' longtime story editor, and workhorse scriptwriters like Jackson Gillis and Seeleg Lester, both of whom served stints as the program's associate producer. But it was still another auteur who gradually emerged as the figure most identified with the program's success. The writers who devised the legal toils in which so many innocents were caught and the legal means by which they could be freed were less important not only than their fictional hero but ultimately than Raymond Burr, the man who embodied the law at its most personal and redemptive.

A signal mark of Burr's growing primacy is the evolution of the credit sequences. Fred Steiner's unforgettable theme music, which is exceptionally successful at evoking both the mood of the series and the tone of its hero, never varies over the program's nine seasons. But the visuals of the show's first four seasons evolve in telling ways, assigning Burr an ever more unrivaled place in court. The first season's credits show him and his costars against a background of courtroom spectators. By the fourth season's credits, the spectators have disappeared along with the four costars. (Interestingly, there is never a trace of Mason's eminently interchangeable clients.) These credits reduce even the judge to a statue, with Burr the only live person present. Subsequent seasons show Burr sitting alone in a deserted courtroom, as if he were the series' sole manifestation of the law.

J. Dennis Bounds has observed that "the character of Mason, as portrayed by Burr, becomes the new author as trademark in each successive media appearance."[13] Anticipating Lorraine Bracco's honoring by the American Psychiatric Association for her work as Dr. Jennifer Melfi on *The Sopranos* (1999–), Burr eventually gave nearly sixty speeches before bar associations and was awarded honorary law degrees from McGeorge College of Law and the University

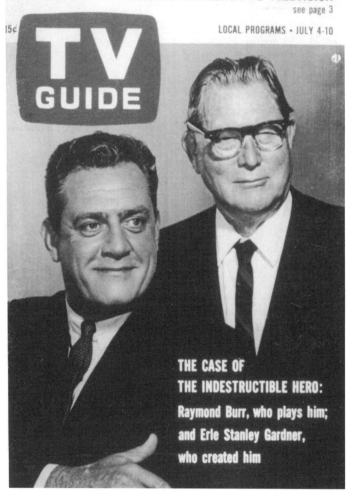

The old auteur of *Perry Mason* (Erle Stanley Gardner, *right*) and the new (Burr).

of New Mexico.[14] In July 1965, two months before the program began its final season, Burr told *TV Guide* interviewer Dwight Whitney that he considered the program and its hero "a public trust" and himself its "chief executor."[15]

But Burr's identification as America's lawyer ran even deeper. As Burr replaced Gardner in the public imagination, Mason displaced Gardner even as the trademark of the original literary franchise. By 1960, the paperback reprint covers that had mentioned Mason's name in smaller type than that of the best-selling Gardner were dwarfing Gardner's name with Mason's. Burr's photograph even began to appear on the lower back cover of these reprints in the place customarily reserved for the author's photo. The implication readers were clearly invited to draw was that just as Burr embodied the legal hero and the legal system that supported him, he embodied the novels on which his adventures were based more compellingly than their author.

Burr took no part in writing, directing, or producing *Perry Mason*—but neither did Gardner. His sole official function as a partner in Paisano Productions was to review each script. Because the people who actually created the series week by week—the screenwriters, directors, and producers—had never been serious candidates for auteurship, the position was Burr's for the taking. He could assume possession of the role not only because he was its most visible exemplar but because he incarnated both the menace and the promise of the American legal system so compellingly. This substitution of one mode of creation for another— incarnation for invention—was an eminently logical outgrowth of the series' attitude toward the law. The law according to Mason was not a network of conflicting imperatives to be constantly reinvigorated by renegotiation but an eternal guarantee of truth, justice, and final exoneration to be re-embodied and celebrated each week. Like Perry Mason,

Perry Mason tops Erle Stanley Gardner. The paperback covers are from (*top row, left to right*) December 1952, April 1954, and November 1957, and (*bottom row, left to right*) November 1959, April 1964, and November 1967.

Mason's authorless, authoritative law simply incarnated the best principles of transcendental moral law.

Once television had set its seal of authorship on Gardner's world, it remained only for the author himself to acknowledge the new model's primacy by imitating it. Although he frequently maintained a critical attitude toward particular episodes in the series, Gardner, as Ian Fleming would do a few years later with the cinematic James Bond, rapidly internalized its formula. The catchy alliterative titles, which Gardner had used sparingly before the television episodes made them ubiquitous, now became his own norm.[16] Burger and Lieutenant Tragg were welcomed into Mason's literary family, rarely to depart. The once optional courtroom finales became obligatory. Beginning with *The Case of the Long-Legged Models* (1958), Gardner even began to incorporate the climactic confessions in open court he had eschewed as frankly unbelievable. In perhaps the ultimate compliment to the series format, Gardner borrowed "The Case of the Spurious Sister," the title of a non-Gardner-based episode that began the show's 1959–60 season, and transformed it into *The Case of the Spurious Spinster*, the title of the Mason novel he published in March 1961. In the process, he even improved the alliteration.

The extent of Burr's ascendancy over both his creators and his fellow cast members is marked most completely by his prominence in "The Perry Mason Game: Case of the Missing Suspect," marketed by Transogram in 1959. The cover of the game's box features Burr's photograph ("Perry Mason as portrayed by Raymond Burr on CBS Television") in no fewer than five places, on every surface capable of displaying an image, and his face looks out from the top of the enclosed instructions as well. Apart from a pair of references buried in a small-print paragraph on opposite sides of the box and a reference at the end of the instructions, "© Paisano Productions, 1959," there is no word of Gardner. Nor does the game mention Barbara Hale, William Hopper, William Talman, Ray Collins, or any of the fictional characters they played onscreen. Mason is the only character apart from the players in the game, and the packaging leaves no doubt that Mason is Raymond Burr. The cover's overview of the game, which describes Mason as "Erle Stanley Gardner's well-known lawyer-detective . . . in books, on radio and TV," accurately reflects the way the game completely inverts his role in Gardner's novels: "The board is an aerial view of the city, and the detectives race in their cars through the city streets, hunting for clues, holding inquests, questioning witnesses, and checking Suspects. The first detective to solve his crime, capture his Suspect, and bring him to the courthouse for trial is the winner." The game's lawyer-detectives, in other words, are given all the functions normally assigned to the police, and the game ends with the successful player's arrival at the courthouse with a suspect whose guilt has already been established. Perry Mason, meet Lieutenant Tragg.

And meet the Father as well. The figure of the "corny, wishy-washy, do-nothing 'Pop'"[17] that prevailed in contemporaneous television sitcoms was widely held to undermine the masculinity of American fathers. Burr's oversized black-and-white photograph on the game box's cover, which occupied the visual position board games typically assigned to the family that would presumably be brought together by playing the game, carried similarly domestic overtones. But the unsmiling Burr, looming over a smaller-scaled color painting of a suspect fleeing the police, united paternal reassurance with patriarchal authority. In this configuration, Burr takes the place of lawyer, detective, police, and author, and indeed

The actor turned auteur, the lawyer turned cop: Burr's face used both to sell "The Perry Mason Game: Case of the Missing Suspect" and to guarantee its acceptance by the family father.

the entire family unit Mason heads in the television series. He provides a model for the family of viewers or players whose group identity could only be confirmed by their salubrious brush with the law. This apotheosis of the performer as auteur would prove an act equally impossible to sustain indefinitely or to follow.

The Defense Rests

The closing episode of *Perry Mason*—a segment appropriately titled "The Case of the Final Fade-Out" and filled with in-jokes like a story about a murder on a film set, the casting of many of the program's longtime employees (from sound and camera technicians to Gail Patrick Jackson), and a judge played in one final spasm of auteurism by Erle Stanley Gardner—aired on 22 May 1966. The series had been in trouble for over a year. Its high production budget was no longer justified by equally high ratings, and in its final season it was horsewhipped by NBC's *Bonanza* (1959–73), a very different kind of family saga. Raymond Burr made no secret of his boredom with the role, and no one at CBS was inclined to fight for it.

The series did not die, however, but passed immediately into the profitable afterlife of syndication. Burr's continuing popularity as Lt. Robert Ironside, another gruff, overbearing, but authoritative detective hero viewers could readily trust, was matched by the success of *Perry Mason* reruns. CBS's attempt to revive the franchise with Monte Markham in *The New Perry Mason* (1973–74), by contrast, was a failure, lasting only fifteen episodes. Many observers ascribed this failure to the absence of Burr and Gardner, who had died in 1971. It might have seemed that Mason's time had passed except in reruns. The crime series that followed were more trendy (*Storefront Lawyers* [CBS, 1970–71]), more clearly attuned to current events and social issues (*Judd for the Defense* [ABC, 1967–69]), and more evocative of a specific sense of place (*The Streets of San Francisco* [ABC, 1972–77]; *Miami Vice* [NBC, 1984–89]). As the season for network programs shrank from 39 to 22 episodes and the running time for one-hour episodes shrank from 52 to 42 minutes, dramatic series grew more hip (*Remington Steele* [NBC, 1982–87]), more self-reflexive (*Moonlighting* [ABC, 1985–89]), and more dependent on ensemble casts rather than a single dominant hero (*Hill Street Blues* [NBC, 1981–87]). Finally, as Elayne Rapping has pointed out, television "cops were largely on the rise and lawyers in decline throughout the 1980s."[1] The 1986 premiere of NBC's *L.A. Law*, with its big cast, multiple plots, story arcs continuing over four to eight episodes, and emphasis on the private lives of its glamour-puss attorneys, might have seemed a repudiation of everything *Perry Mason* had stood for.

But there was still an appetite for Mason, as NBC confirmed when its broadcast of the two-hour made-for-television movie "Perry Mason Returns" on 1 December 1985 won a Nielsen rating of 27.2, capturing an estimated 39 percent of the viewers watching television during its time slot, to become the most-watched program that week.[2] Although the film had not been planned to inaugurate a series, its success soon encouraged its creators, writer/producer Dean Hargrove and producer Fred Silverman, to launch a stream of two-hour sequels at the rate of two to four a year over the next ten years. Most of these were nearly as successful commercially as Mason's initial return. They are especially valuable for the light they throw on the formula of the CBS series and its subsequent evolution.

Although the entertainment industry is notorious for repackaging and recycling its most valuable commodities, the resurrection of Mason in the 1980s must have seemed even riskier than the original television series. After all, Mason would be competing not only with many other more timely crime shows and indeed his own syndicated reruns but a world in which the status of lawyers had changed dramatically. The legal profession had undergone a serious crisis of confidence since the Watergate scandal. As presidential attorney John Dean noted in his testimony to the investigating committee about preparing a list of targets likely to be indicted, "My first reaction was there certainly are an awful lot of lawyers involved here."[3] The period of the Watergate investigation, which coincided almost exactly with the failure of *The New Perry Mason*, was clearly not the ideal time to launch a series about a heroic attorney. But the stains on the legal profession continued beyond President Richard Nixon's resignation. Public-opinion polls continued to place lawyers among the most distrusted professionals in America, and lawyer jokes flourished. (What do you call a thousand lawyers at the bottom of the ocean? A good beginning.) Once the progressive social engineers of the 1950s and 1960s, attorneys were reviled as hairsplitting shysters interested only in preserving the wealth of their corporate clients or augmenting their own by solicitous attention to their billable hours. Years before *A Few Good Men* (1992), *The Firm* (1993), and *Erin Brockovich* (2000) reflected the depth of America's disillusionment with lawyers, . . . *And Justice for All* (1979) depicted an utterly dysfunctional justice system in freefall, and *The Verdict* (1982) set an alcoholic loser of a plaintiff's attorney against a conspiracy stretching from courthouses to hospitals to the archdiocese of Boston.

It was in this antilegalistic climate that Viacom, which had purchased the rights to Gardner's hero, sought to revive Perry Mason. From the very beginning, the series played on public disdain for lawyers. Just as Watergate had made a national hero of elderly North Carolina senator Sam Ervin, the widespread suspicion of lawyers created an opening for a heroic antilawyer who could capture the hearts of the public by trouncing other lawyers more lawyerly than he was.

The task of "Perry Mason Returns" and its successors was simplified by the fact that as inimical as lawyers may have become to a public that associated them with White House cover-ups and criminal defenses of the indefensible, there were worse things. Crime had become a far more worrisome social problem since the 1950s. Throughout the 1960s television had offered as a counterpoint to Perry Mason the threat of social meltdown via civil rights demonstrations, big-city riots, and antiwar protests. Fear of crime was actively promoted by television networks' belief that "the surest bet for luring viewers away from their competitors [was] to switch their programming priorities . . . toward an almost exclusive emphasis on crime, sleaze, mysterious 'unsolved' tragedies, and the like."[4]

Such fears are evoked from the opening scene of "Perry Mason Returns," a horror-film pastiche that presents computer tycoon Arthur Gordon (Patrick O'Neal) saying good night to his executive assistant and venturing out into a dark and stormy night. Gordon is followed home by a stalker, eventually identified as Bobby Lynch (James Kidnie), who pulls up alongside him at a traffic light, turns his radio up to harass him, and playfully cocks his finger at Gordon as if to shoot him. The echo of "The Case of the Moth-Eaten Mink" and "The Case of the Restless Redhead" is unmistakable. Just as important, but harder to notice, is the fact that this is virtually the first time since those first televised cases that the program opens with a character being physically threatened, however playfully. And unlike Dixie Dayton and Evelyn Bagby in those earlier episodes, Gordon really is about to be killed by the man who threatens him. Returning to a deserted home, Gordon takes out a gun when he hears a suspicious noise, only to be surprised by the relatives gathered to celebrate his birthday. Even this episode darkens with Gordon's revelation that he intends to cut all three of his children out of his will and replace his wife as the head of his charitable foundation. The following sequence presents something the original series had hardly ever shown directly: Gordon's murder by a figure easily identifiable as Lynch but tricked out in a woman's dress and wig in order to pass among witnesses as Della Street, the executive assistant Gordon has nominated to head his foundation.

The main concern of this opening sequence is to create a dangerous world—not dangerous in general, but dangerous to one specific character about to be killed. (Throughout the episode, physical danger will be associated exclusively with the presence of Lynch.) Instead of leading viewers gradually through a web of problematic relationships, "Perry Mason Returns" presents all the leading suspects in a single scene and emphasizes not the complexity and variety of their relationships to the murder victim but their simplicity and similarity. In addition, the film, taking advantage of relaxed television guidelines for the presentation of onscreen violence, restores the *to pathos* the earlier cases had erased. "Perry Mason Returns" shows not only Gordon's murder but the events surrounding it, from the stalker's waiting outside his office to his later movements in planting evidence that will incriminate Della at the murder scene and in her home.

In fact, the camera continues to take an unprecedented visual interest in the assassin up to the moment he is killed.

Showing these murders onscreen satisfies the sensationalist appetites of a less tender generation of television audiences while apparently diminishing the capacity for surprise. The model for showing the killer at work is *Columbo* (NBC, 1971–77), every episode of which begins by presenting a murder whose perpetrator is known to the audience but not to Lieutenant Columbo (Peter Falk). But now, as in several of Mason's two-hour sequels, the killer has merely been hired by the real culprit, the family intimate with access and motive. Hence that culprit's identity can remain a teasing secret even as his triggerman can be dispatched in another *to pathos* when the news of his involvement threatens his client. More generally, the telemovies place considerably more emphasis on physical action. "Perry Mason Returns" contains two stalking sequences, two car-chase sequences, and several near misses among the criminals, their accomplices, and the detective Mason hires to work the case.

Such obvious differences would seem to call for a different kind of hero. The whole allure of Mason, however, is that he is the pole star in a fallen world, the one thing that remains exactly the same. The structure of the episode, despite its two-hour length, deliberately evokes the structure of Mason's one-hour cases far more closely than the structure of any contemporaneous feature-length crime film, casting Mason as an anachronistic survivor of the 1950s. When the police predictably arrest Della, Mason visits her in prison with the news that he has resigned from the appellate court to defend her. Lawyers may have changed over the years, but Mason has not, in no small part because he has been a judge, not a lawyer. With this stroke, his return can take advantage of the American public's enduring respect for judges from

Watergate jurist John J. Sirica to Hon. Joseph A. Wapner, whose twelve-year run on the syndicated reality program *The People's Court* had begun in 1981. Even the obvious physical changes in Burr since 1966—his gray hair and beard, his heavier, more gravelly voice, his lumbering gait and slower movements—simply make him more courtly and avuncular than ever.

Mason is the perfect champion for a client whose innocence is heavily overdetermined. Even if Della Street (still played by Barbara Hale) could murder somebody, the audience knows she didn't murder Arthur Gordon, because she would hardly hire a killer who would turn around and frame her. Della's patent innocence releases Mason from his customary obligation to cross-examine his client. Instead he blossoms into a knight-errant who can take her hand in one scene and hug her in another, inflecting their reunion with the audience's nostalgia for the good old days when lawyers were all as trustworthy as judges, or as Perry Mason. For the first time in his long career as Perry Mason, Burr is playing Mason not as a powerful plot function and authoritative avatar of the justice system but as a character with conventionally dramatic emotions.

The downside of Mason's status as courtly anachronism—his inability to get around easily—requires a more active assistant than Paul Drake, and he gets one in Paul Drake, Jr. (William Katt, replaced as Mason's sidekick after the third season by William R. Moses as the more polished attorney Ken Malansky). Sax-playing, dune-buggy-driving Paul is everything Mason is not. He runs his one-man agency so inattentively that his phone is about to be cut off. He is brash, impulsive, and more boyish than William Hopper ever thought of being. If Mason has become an antilawyer, Paul is an antidetective who regularly fails to secure crucial evidence. Even the final incriminating statement from an accomplice turns out to be Paul's unpaid phone bill.

Mason constantly expresses skepticism about whether Paul is "ready for this one." Paul responds by complaining, "Why am I getting the third degree here?" And Mason refuses to tell Paul he's done a good job until the very last line of the film. The result is to create a salt-and-pepper double hero. Paul engages in activities that are visually much more interesting than Mason's—it is he who repeatedly confronts the bad guys directly—and he gets just as much screen time, since it would be unthinkable to choreograph any of the obligatory action sequences intended to lure younger audiences around Raymond Burr.

In what would become a subtle private joke running through the new series of telemovies, neither Mason nor Paul is entirely of this world. Mason is too chivalric, anachronistic, principled, and sentimental to correspond to mid-1980s notions of lawyerly behavior. And Paul is too raffish, cublike, and transparently sincere in the many roles he assumes (insurance adjuster, solar-power inspector, non-denominational minister) that are the closest the telemovies come to Burr's legalistic end runs in the older series. Together they neatly box in Julie Scott (Cassie Yates), the deputy district attorney designed as a magnet for the audience's contempt toward lawyers. From the moment the D.A. introduces the deputy who will be trying Della—"It's not a him, it's a her. Times have changed"—she is associated with a rough-and-tumble present with which Mason's courtly invocation of a vanished past can be favorably contrasted.[5] Unlike Mason, whose sole interest is in seeing Della vindicated, Scott approaches the trial as a welcome battle of wits. "This is going to be fun. It would be better if he were at the top of his game, but he's still Perry Mason," she tells her boss smugly. Scott is not only a woman, initially dressed in clothes so mannish that she seems paired more closely with Lynch in drag than Mason, but an arrogant upstart disrespectful of an elder she should revere. Replacing Yates with

David Ogden Stiers as Denver District Attorney Michael Reston in the next eight telemovies alleviates the obvious sexism of the contest between the two lawyers while still maintaining the hint of generational and temperamental contrast.

A commonplace of television series stretched to feature length on the big or small screen is that they are padded. True to form, the Mason telemovies have their share of unnecessary and overextended scenes. What is more surprising, however, is what they minimize: the suspects and the courtroom. "Perry Mason Returns" allows Mason only one conversation with each of the principal suspects. In the most extended of these, he swiftly reduces Gordon's widow, Paula (Holland Taylor), to such furious accusations against Della that family attorney Kenneth Braddock (Richard Anderson) warns her what will happen if she repeats the performance in court. In his briefer exchanges with each of the Gordon children, Mason simply demands their alibis for the time Lynch was shot and taxes them with incriminating secrets he usually knows already rather than seeking to uncover new evidence. He taunts David with his gambling debts and Laura with her husband's infidelities before his visit to Kathryn reveals that she is involved with Braddock—the only discovery Mason makes on his own in two hours.

The courtroom sequence is even more remarkable for its omissions. Virtually all the witnesses who testify are justice-system functionaries or minor characters. Mason hammers at them without any result except to provoke the prosecutor's weary outburst when Mason dresses a male stuntman as a woman in order to impeach a witness who placed Della at the scene: "The days of these theatrics are long since gone. Mr. Mason is trying to compensate for his lack of any plausible defense by turning this courtroom into a sideshow." There is no significant interaction between Mason and any possible culprit until he puts Paula and Kathryn on the stand, arguing again with the prosecutor rather than the witnesses. The entire courtroom sequence takes considerably less time than the corresponding sequence in a typical one-hour episode. Nor does it present a coherent counternarrative of the case. Mason merely aims to sow doubt until he obtains crucial evidence. The sequence is intercut with Paul's more active quest for that evidence. The film thus offers a double climax in which Paul and Mason perform as equal partners. The one pretends to dig up the crucial evidence, the other pretends to display it in court as he hammers home his bluff in an irresistible litany of questions familiar from the CBS series: "Isn't is true . . . Isn't it true . . . Isn't it true . . . ?"

In addition to giving no special emphasis to either the suspects or the setting or conventions of the courtroom, "Perry Mason Returns" provides little in the way of mystery, since the identity of Lynch's murderous client cannot be inferred by either Mason or the audience on the basis of the evidence that is presented. Only Paul's offscreen revelation, Lynch's father's unheard answer to his question, "Who said that I did [shoot your son]?" identifies the killer as Kenneth Braddock. If the episode seems deficient in logic, however, that is because its logic, like that of contemporaneous crime series as different as *Remington Steele, Miami Vice*, and *Moonlighting*, is so largely intertextual rather than textual. All its richest meanings are reserved for viewers familiar with the formula of the one-hour program, even though its departures from that formula are what invoke the comparison. It is hard to imagine how anyone unfamiliar with the CBS series could accept the elephantine byplay between Mason and Della, the brusque but unprobing way he questions suspects on and off the stand, his instant personal rivalry with the prosecutor, his constant criticism of his own investigator, and the film's many in-jokes. Della constantly tells Mason what a great boss he used to be, and he just as frequently asserts her innocence with a conviction he had never lavished on any previous client. Paul, wounded by Mason's lack of respect for his abilities, protests that "Della means too much to me" for him to do any less than his best, and Della comes early to a meeting so that she can clean Paul's untidy office—thoroughly appropriate behavior for real-life mother and son Barbara Hale and William Katt. Finally, Richard Anderson, who plays Braddock, the Gordon family's murderous attorney, would have been familiar to fans of the original television series as Lt. Steve Drumm, Tragg's replacement in its final season. His double status as an old acquaintance of Mason's and a former series regular, which apparently shield him from suspicion, are simply a setup for the film to show what it really thinks of lawyers who aren't Perry Mason.

Indeed, the principal ingenuity of the Mason telemovies that followed was their unlikely casting of defendants, victims, and killers. Sister Margaret (Michele Greene) is accused of murdering Father Tom O'Neil (Timothy Bottoms) in "The Case of the Notorious Nun" (25 May 1986). Steve Carr, the abrasive talk-show host in "The Case of the Shooting Star" (9 November 1986), is played by Alan Thicke, the abrasive host of *The Alan Thicke Show* (1980) and *Thicke of the Night* (1983–84). Glenn Robertson (Gene Barry), the husband of Mason's onetime love Laura Kilgallen (Jean Simmons), is accused of murder in "The Case of the Lost Love" (23 February 1987)—a complication the film tops when it reveals that Laura herself is the killer. Mason defends a hockey player (Jason Beghe) accused of killing his team's owner (Pernell Roberts) in "The Case of the All-Star Assassin" (19 November 1989), a gang leader (Michael Nader) accused of killing his long-suffering wife in "The Case of the Maligned Mobster" (11 February 1991), and the consort (Patrick O'Neal, the victim in "Perry Mason Returns") accused of killing his cosmetics-queen wife (Morgan Fairchild, playing an extraordinarily well-preserved sixty-two-year-old) in "The Case of the Skin-Deep Scandal" (19 February 1993). More generally, the telemovies systematically root their surprises in finding new functions for formulaic elements familiar from the CBS series.

Eventually the telemovies outgrew the need to justify Mason's return as the lawyer who could be trusted because he wasn't a lawyer, mitigated the personal rivalries between him and a series of luckless prosecutors, attended more seriously to their mystery elements, and began to spend proportionately more time in the courtroom. But their conventions remained distinctive. Mason, no longer a disinterested seek-

Patrick O'Neal, murdered as Arthur Gordon in "Perry Mason Returns," rises from the dead to play accused wife-killer Arthur Westbrook, flanked by Della and Mason, in "The Case of the Skin-Deep Scandal" (19 February 1993).

er of truth and justice, is a paterfamilias who typically has some long-standing connection to the defendant. The tele-movies continue to show the murders the CBS series had avoided. Suspects are created in parallel groups and devel-oped in parallel scenes. And the final courtroom climax is demoted permanently to half a climax it shares with the sidekick's more active pursuit of crucial evidence that brings him up against henchmen as visually distinctive as Bobby Lynch. In Burr's final outing, "The Case of the Killer Kiss" (29 November 1993), Mason, having left the courtroom in response to an urgent summons, turns up in a single, high-ly atypical shot in the action sequence just in time to rescue Ken Malansky from a shootout with a corrupt sheriff and his confused deputy.

All these elements remain in place throughout this final episode, beginning when Kris Buckner (Genie Francis) is arrested for poisoning Mark Stratton (Sean Kanan), her treacherous and highly allergic costar in the daytime drama *Mile High*. Mark has been killed by the ingenious technique of adding walnut oil to the lipstick of his new costar and fiancée, Charlotte Grant, and replacing his anti-allergen with more walnut oil.[6] Mason, an old family friend with whom Kris has lost touch because she knows he sided with her late parents in their disapproval of her acting career, agrees to defend her. Since the burden of the episode's opening move-ment is how exclusively the evidence points at Kris, Mason's task is to turn the other members of the program's cast and crew into suspects. Accordingly, he attacks the gatekeeper's testimony that Kris was the only person who could have entered Mark's dressing room the preceding night to exchange his injector of epinephrine for one filled with wal-nut oil. He asks all the other cast members about their whereabouts that night. And he digs up information that provides them all with motives as powerful as Kris's own.

Mason is never shown digging up any of this information or even seeking it. The telefilms had long farmed out the need to dig up information to supporting characters like Michelle Benti (Wendy Crewson), the providential tabloid reporter in "The Case of the Shooting Star" who offers to trade Paul information in return for his access to the closed movie set on which the leading suspects are working. Mason's scenes with each member of the cast or crew follow an identical pattern. He begins with a few leading remarks, indicates that he knows the secret that gives the suspect a motive, and demands particulars of an alibi which he then proceeds to break, again without ever gathering evidence. Although Mason's conversations with suspects in his salad days had been formulaic, these more forthrightly challenging conversations are so much more formulaic that they are essentially interchangeable.

A still more important departure of the telemovies is that Mason is presented not as a discoverer of truth but as a man of wisdom. Even when he does not know the facts of the case, he knows that Kris is as innocent as Della Street "because I've known you since you were a baby." When he examines witnesses in court, he never needs to get them to reveal anything he does not already know. The courtroom thus changes from a place where the truth is discovered to a place where the truth, or what the defense attorney knows to be the truth, is revealed, and Mason from a person who seeks the truth to a person who knows it.

Raymond Burr died shortly before filming of this final episode was completed,[7] and after four attempts to continue the franchise, one with Paul Sorvino as attorney Nick Caruso and three with Hal Holbrook as attorney Wild Bill McKenzie substituting for Burr, NBC laid the series to rest. Both of Burr's designated replacements were accomplished actors with extensive experience on television series (Sorvino on *The Oldest Rookie* [CBS, 1987–88] and *Law &*

Mason's last case: Raymond Burr in the posthumously released "The Case of the Killer Kiss" (29 November 1993).

Order, Holbrook on *Designing Women* [CBS, 1986–89] and *Evening Shade* [CBS, 1990–94]). But neither supplanted him or effaced his memory, for the times demanded not just Mason but Burr as Mason.

The reasons why are instructive. Concluding his comprehensive study of "Perry Mason as a transmedia narrative," published shortly after the last of the Holbrook episodes aired, J. Dennis Bounds wondered, "Was Burr

Mason? . . . Is it the formula or Burr that made the series run?"[8] Now that question can be definitively answered by the networks' decision not to revive the franchise with another character (Sorvino and Holbrook as substitutes for Mason) or another performer (Monte Markham as the new Perry Mason). Burr was indeed Mason. Once the mantle of series auteur had passed from Erle Stanley Gardner to his handpicked star, it remained with him and will probably remain with him forever. But why was Burr the only possible Mason? The short answer, of course, is that he was not. Warren William, Ricardo Cortez, and Donald Woods, along with John Larkin and several other radio performers, all had a crack at the role before Burr came along. Nor is there any reason to assume that Fred MacMurray, Efrem Zimbalist, Jr., or Mike Connors, all of whom went on to successful television careers, would not have been equally well suited for the role. Yet Burr became such a definitive Mason that it became as unthinkable to recast the role as it would have been to ask a new actress to read for I Love Lucy (1951–57).

The success of the later telemovies confirms the pivotal importance of Burr as auteur. The continuing popularity of Burr's Mason long after the graying, frog-voiced, generally immobile star, playing out his greatest role in a series of increasingly formulaic scripts, no longer looked, sounded, moved, or acted like Mason, indicates the extent to which Mason's impact had become iconographic, symbolic, and self-reflexive. Long after the floodtide of America's affection for lawyers had passed, Burr continued to incarnate the role regardless of how he looked or acted because the ways Mason looked or acted were less important than the values with which Burr had become associated. Thirty years after he first essayed the role, Burr was still America's lawyer, the palpable guarantee that the nation's legal system, however threatening and aloof, was fair and accessible. The opaque yet reassuring hero who had been devised as an expression of Gardner's franchise control and marketed by CBS as a sign of their gravitas and integrity during the crucial transition from stand-alone drama to formulaic series drama had been transformed precisely because of his resistance to change. Once the incarnation of both the patriarchal threat and the paternal covenant of American justice, Mason had become a nostalgic promise that the all-too-political history of the nation's legal system was actually rooted in the personal history of a single beloved star. Burr's renascence as a full-blown character actor signaled that integrity, aggressiveness, and dedication to the law and one's clients abided in that system, even more conventionally humanized, at a time of its lowest public esteem. Lucky enough to outlive a seismic shift in America's attitude toward lawyers, Burr aged into the anachronistic 1950s lawyer equally aging baby boomers yearned for most powerfully.

99

In an era marked equally by suspicion of lawyers and judges and courts and fascination with them—think only of Judge Judy, Court TV, and *Bush v. Gore*—Burr's Mason remains a potent figure to this day. The figure he incarnated represents not so much a vision as an everlasting hope for the legal system no other performer now has the history of associations to revive. No wonder the final Holbrook episode's credits ended with the promise: "The Last Perry Mason Mystery."

Introduction

1. There were thirty such two-hour telefilms, but the last four, although they were titled "A Perry Mason Mystery," were made after Burr's death and did not feature Mason but attorneys Nick Caruso (Paul Sorvino) and Wild Bill McKenzie (Hal Holbrook).

2. Brian Kelleher and Diana Merrill, *The Perry Mason TV Show Book: The Complete Story of America's Favorite Television Lawyer by Two of His Greatest Fans* (New York: St. Martin's, 1987), 26.

3. Ibid., 70.

4. Lau had appeared on the series twice before, once as Anderson at Tragg's side in "The Case of the Unwelcome Bride" (16 December 1961), and once even earlier, as Mason's client Amory Fallon in "The Case of the Impatient Partner" (16 September 1961).

5. This book offers no empirical documentation of the program's effects on audiences because its run ended before television researchers began to gather the relevant data. The consensual conclusion about law enforcement programs since *Perry Mason* has been, as James M. Carlson puts it in *Prime Time Law Enforcement: Crime Show Viewing and Attitudes toward the Criminal Justice System* (New York: Praeger, 1985), that they "put forth a 'crime control' point of view that is highly supportive of the status quo and conventional views of proper behavior, ethics, and morality" (52). See also George Gerbner and Larry Gross, "Living with Television: The Violence Profile," *Journal of*

Communication 26 (1976): 173–99; Steven Stark, "Perry Mason Meets Sonny Crockett: The History of Lawyers and the Police as Television Heroes," *University of Miami Law Review* 42 (1987): 229–83; Mallory Wober and Barrie Gunter, *Television and Social Control* (New York: St. Martin's, 1988), 20–52; and Aaron Doyle, "'Cops': Television Reality as Policing Reality," in *Entertaining Crime: Television Reality Programs*, ed. Mark Fishman and Gray Cavender (New York: de Gruyter, 1998), 95–116.

Chapter 1

1. Sigmund Freud, "Creative Writers and Day-Dreaming" (1908), in *The Standard Edition of the Complete Psychological Works of Sigmund Freud*, trans. and ed. James Strachey (London: Hogarth, 1959), 9:150.

2. John G. Cawelti, *Adventure, Mystery, and Romance: Formula Stories as Art and Popular Culture* (Chicago: University of Chicago Press, 1976), 35.

3. See, for example, the characterizations in Robert Graves and Alan Hodge, *The Long Week End: A Social History of Great Britain, 1918–1939* (New York: Macmillan, 1941), 290; Raymond Chandler, "The Simple Art of Murder," *Later Novels and Other Writings* (New York: Library of America, 1995), 977–87; and Colin Watson, *Snobbery with Violence: Crime Stories and Their Audience* (London: Eyre and Spottiswoode, 1971), 95–107.

4. The story is largely responsible for the widespread and erroneous belief that a dead body is necessary to warrant a murder charge, though Post, like Gardner a practicing attorney, is careful through Mason to distinguish between a body and the body of a crime—the compelling evidence, whether or not it includes a corpse, that a crime has been committed.

5. Melville Davisson Post, *The Man of Last Resort: or, The Clients of Randolph Mason* (New York: Putnam, 1897), 253. Interestingly, when the amoral Mason switched sides in his third volume of short stories, *The Corrector of Destinies* (1908), to right wrongs for the luckless by using equally recondite legal points and procedures, the underlying formula of his stories changed remarkably little.

6. For an entertaining account of some of Gardner's own real-life courtroom shenanigans, see Alva Johnston, *The Case of Erle Stanley Gardner* (New York: Morrow, 1947), 20–24, 58–70.

7. For Moore's bibliography, see Dorothy B. Hughes, *Erle Stanley*

Gardner: The Case of the Real Perry Mason (New York: Morrow, 1978), 312–41. A representative recent collection of Gardner's early pulp writing is *The Danger Zone and Other Stories* (Norfolk, VA: Crippen and Landru, 2004).

8. Hughes, *Erle Stanley Gardner*, 123, 124.

9. Johnston, *The Case of Erle Stanley Gardner*, 15.

10. Elmore Leonard, "Writers on Writing: Easy on the Adverbs, Exclamation Points and Especially Hooptedoodle," *New York Times*, 16 July 2001, sec. E, p. 1.

11. Hughes, *Erle Stanley Gardner*, 73.

12. Other films in the series include *The Case of the Lucky Legs* (1935), *The Case of the Black Cat* (1936), starring Ricardo Cortez as Mason, and *The Case of the Stuttering Bishop* (1937), starring Donald Woods.

13. Hughes, *Erle Stanley Gardner*, 241.

14. J. Dennis Bounds, *Perry Mason: The Authorship and Reproduction of a Popular Hero,* Contributions to the Study of Popular Culture 56 (Westport, CT: Greenwood, 1996), 85.

15. The longest radio segment of the program, "The Sinister Sister," ran for over fifteen months, from 27 October 1947 to 8 February 1949. The shortest, "The Baby's Shoes," was confined to a single fifteen-minute episode broadcast on 15 April 1946.

16. Hughes, *Erle Stanley Gardner*, 243.

17. Kelleher and Merrill, *The Perry Mason TV Show Book*, 32.

18. Burr's homosexuality was well known in the Hollywood community despite his three reputed marriages.

19. Kelleher and Merrill, *The Perry Mason TV Show Book*, 15.

20. See William Boddy, *Fifties Television: The Industry and Its Critics* (Urbana: University of Illinois Press, 1990), 188–89.

21. Erik Barnouw, *The Image Empire* (New York: Oxford University Press, 1970), 26.

22. Lynn Spigel, "The Making of a TV Literate Elite," in *The Television Studies Book*, ed. Christine Geraghty and David Lusted (London: Arnold, 1998), 63–85, at 87. For a fuller discussion of these scandals and the resulting sense of crisis throughout the networks, see Boddy, *Fifties Television*, 214–32.

23. "Sponsor Scope," *Sponsor*, 6 April 1957, 9.

Chapter 2

1. Quoted in Hughes, *Erle Stanley Gardner*, 251.

2. In "The Case of the Restless Redhead," Burger notes that Mason

is "attempting to cross-examine his own witness." In "The Case of the Nervous Accomplice" (5 October 1957), Burger remarks, "Counsel is up to his usual grandstanding." In "The Case of the Sulky Girl" (19 October 1957), he complains that Mason "is making a mockery of this courtroom." In rural Logan City, District Attorney Harry Cortland charges, "You're trying to use this court as a stage for some of your well-known theatrics" ("The Case of the Drowning Duck" [12 October 1957]). These outbursts all came in the program's first month on the air.

3. Gardner occasionally considered varying the formula. Although he never seriously entertained the prospect of Mason's losing a case, he was at least open to discussing less drastic changes. In *Erle Stanley Gardner*, Hughes describes an episode in February 1961, midway through the program's fourth season, when "he entertained the idea of putting a young assistant in Mason's office, to appeal to the younger generation, and also to bring in a love interest, which he continued to reject for Della and Perry" (250). Citing early opposition from his publishers to a formula that was obviously still enjoying a large audience, however, Gardner ultimately vetoed any change.

4. John Ellis, *Visible Fictions: Cinema: Television: Video*, rev. ed. (London: Routledge, 1992), 135. In *Prime-Time Television: Content and Control*, 2nd ed. (Newbury Park, CA: Sage, 1992), Muriel G. and Joel M. Cantor note that for such social theorists as Max Horkheimer, T. W. Adorno, and Herbert Marcuse, "the central fact of capitalist civilization was the progressive collapse of the family as an adequate socializing agent; its mediating function has been passed on to the culture industries" (91). Hence, as Diane F. Alters notes in Stewart M. Hoover et al., *Media, Home, and Family* (London: Routledge, 2004), "in keeping with [its] presence in the family home, television's imagery is overtly familial" (55). For an especially penetrating discussion of the relation between television's representation of families and its conception of the families who watched it, see Lynn Spigel, *Make Room for TV: Television and the Family Ideal in Postwar America* (Chicago: University of Chicago Press, 1992).

5. Mason is not always charming to children either. Accused of tampering with evidence in "The Case of the Demure Defendant" (4 January 1958), he responds by cross-examining Arthur Lindner (Rickie Sorensen), the young boy he got to dive for the saccharine

bottle that may or may not have held poison.

Chapter 3

1. See John Fiske, *Television Culture* (London: Methuen, 1987), 28, 32.

2. Raymond Burr had an average of 80 percent of the dialogue over the life of the series, according to Kelleher and Merrill, *The Perry Mason TV Show Book*, 38.

3. John Corner, *Critical Ideas in Television Studies* (Oxford: Clarendon, 1999), 58.

4. Sam Frank, *Buyer's Guide to 50 Years of TV on Video* (Amherst, NY: Prometheus, 1999), 957.

5. Kelleher and Merrill, *The Perry Mason TV Show Book*, 22.

6. W. H. Lewis, "Witness for the Prosecution," *TV Guide*, 30 November 1974, 5–7.

7. The only client of Mason's who ever testifies on her own behalf, Janice Barton (Julie Adams) in "The Case of the Deadly Verdict" (3 October 1963), is the only client who is found guilty.

8. Arthur Miller, *Miller's Court* (Boston: Houghton Mifflin, 1982), 287.

9. Elayne Rapping, *Law and Justice as Seen on TV* (New York: New York University Press, 2003), 47.

10. Richard Dyer, *Only Entertainment* (London: Routledge, 1992), 24.

11. Jürgen Habermas, *The Structural Transformation of the Public Sphere: An Inquiry into a Category of Bourgeois Society*, trans. Thomas Burger with the assistance of Frederick Lawrence (Cambridge, MA: MIT Press, 1989), 195.

12. Carlson, *Prime Time Law Enforcement*, 117, 2.

13. Wende Vyborney Dumble, "And Justice for All: The Messages behind 'Real' Courtroom Dramas," in *Television Studies: Textual Analysis*, ed. Gary Burns and Robert J. Thompson (New York: Praeger, 1989), 103–18, at 116.

Chapter 4

1. David Marc and Robert J. Thompson, *Prime Time, Prime Movers: From I Love Lucy to L.A. Law—America's Greatest TV Shows and the People Who Created Them* (Boston: Little, Brown, 1992), 7. The point was first established by Muriel Cantor in *The Hollywood TV Producer* (New York: Basic Books, 1971).

2. Marc and Thompson, *Prime Time, Prime Movers*, 117.

3. Hughes, *Erle Stanley Gardner*, 247.

4. Erle Stanley Gardner, *The Case of the Silent Partner* (1940; rpt. New York: Pocket Books, 1948), 25.

5. Paisano passed over only three of Gardner's sixty-eight novels before 1963: *The Case of the Counterfeit Eye* (1935), *The Case of the Golddigger's Purse* (1945), and *The Case of the Glamorous Ghost* (1955). Oddly, Gardner's first novel, *The Case of the Velvet Claws* (1933), was one of the last to be adapted for television (21 March 1963).

6. This advantage gradually disappeared over the life of the series. All the episodes based on new Gardner novels from "The Case of the Daring Decoy" (29 March 1958) to "The Case of the Mystified Miner" (24 February 1962, based on *The Case of the Spurious Spinster*) aired at least a year before the date of their first paperback publication. As the program's appetite for scripts became more voracious and the production window between Gardner's hardcover and paperback editions narrowed, this margin narrowed as well and ultimately reversed. "The Case of the Bigamous Spouse" (14 November 1963), "The Case of the Blonde Bonanza" (17 December 1964), and "The Case of the Mischievous Doll" (13 May 1965) all followed their paperback editions by several months.

7. This roster of future stars includes Robert Redford, Angie Dickinson, Burt Reynolds, Louise Fletcher, Ryan O'Neal, Cloris Leachman, Leonard Nimoy, Barbara Eden, Norman Fell, Gavin MacLeod, Jerry Van Dyke, Frances Bavier, Adam West, Gary Collins, Daniel J. Travanti, Barbara Bain, Werner Klemperer, and Ellen Burstyn (billed under the name Ellen McRae).

8. Bounds, *Perry Mason*, 116. In the following season, Burr's place was taken twice more by guest attorneys Joe Kelly (Mike Connors) in "The Case of the Bullied Bowler" (5 November 1964) and Ken Kramer (Barry Sullivan) in "The Case of the Thermal Thief" (14 January 1965).

9. In introducing this segment in the 1992 TBS retrospective, Barbara Hale explained that it was part of an experiment CBS undertook in filming individual episodes of the network's most popular series in color.

10. These episodes, almost always based on Gardner's novels, include "The Case of the Silent Partner" (26 October 1957) and "The Case of the Baited Hook" (21 December 1957).

11. Laurence Marks, who had cowritten "The Case of the Moth-Eaten Mink," noted years later that "ratings went really high as soon as you hit the courtroom." See Jim Davidson, "Writing the Perry Mason Pilot: Interviews with TV Writers Ben Starr and Laurence Marks," *National Association for the Advancement of Perry Mason Newsletter*, no. 46 (winter 1990–91): 9, quoted in Bounds, *Perry Mason*, 127.

12. Such shots, virtually nonexistent in the series' first season and rare throughout most of its second, become a regular feature in the 1959–60 season and rapidly assume the status of the series' most durable visual cliché.

13. Bounds, *Perry Mason*, 156.

14. Kelleher and Merrill, *The Perry Mason TV Show Book*, 42; Hughes, *Erle Stanley Gardner*, 292.

15. Dwight Whitney, "Pleading His Own Case," in *TV Guide: The First 25 Years*, ed. Jay S. Harris (New York: Simon and Schuster, 1978), 113.

16. Of the 54 Mason novels Gardner published through 1957, 26, just under half, have alliterative titles. Of the 28 Mason novels he published from 1958 through 1973, 18 are alliterative. Of the 203 television episodes that do not borrow their titles from Gardner, 162 are alliterative.

17. Spigel, *Make Room for TV*, 65.

Conclusion

1. Rapping, *Law and Justice as Seen on TV*, 3.

2. Bounds, *Perry Mason*, 155.

3. The Watergate and Related Activities, Phase I: Watergate Investigation, S Res. 60, Senate Select Committee on Presidential Campaign Activities, Presidential Campaign Activities of 1972, Book 3 (25 and 26 June 1973), 1013.

4. Rapping, *Law and Justice as Seen on TV*, 258.

5. The film pits Mason against the post-Watergate view of lawyers more directly when Lynch, unhappy that Mason has taken on Della's defense, phones his unseen client in panic: "You knew all about her. Who'd you think she was gonna get, Nixon?"

6. Most cast members of *Mile High* are played by well-known soap-opera stars, including Karen Moncrieff (*Days of Our Lives, Santa Barbara*), Arleen Sorkin (*Days of Our Lives*), Krista Tesreau (*The Guiding Light, Santa Barbara*), Linda Dano (*Another World, One*

Life to Live), Stuart Damon (*General Hospital*), and Genie Francis, whose role as Laura Gray Vining Webber Baldwin Cassadine Spencer in *General Hospital* made her the most famous soap-opera star in America, and one whose oft-married character would be easiest for Mason to disapprove of.

7. The shot in which Mason, seen from behind, hurriedly leaves the courtroom on his way to rescue Ken had to be filmed with a double.

8. Bounds, *Perry Mason*, 155, 157.

BIBLIOGRAPHY

Barnouw, Erik. *The Image Empire*. New York: Oxford University Press, 1970.

Boddy, William. *Fifties Television: The Industry and Its Critics*. Urbana: University of Illinois Press, 1990.

Bounds, J. Dennis. *Perry Mason: The Authorship and Reproduction of a Popular Hero*. Contributions to the Study of Popular Culture 56. Westport, CT: Greenwood, 1996.

Burns, Gary, and Robert J. Thompson. *Television Studies: Textual Analysis*. New York: Praeger, 1989.

Cantor, Muriel G. *The Hollywood TV Producer*. New York: Basic Books, 1971.

Cantor, Muriel G., and Joel M. Cantor. *Prime-Time Television: Content and Control*. 2nd ed. Newbury Park, CA: Sage, 1992.

Carlson, James M. *Prime Time Law Enforcement: Crime Show Viewing and Attitudes toward the Criminal Justice System*. New York: Praeger, 1985.

Cawelti, John G. *Adventure, Mystery, and Romance: Formula Stories as Art and Popular Culture*. Chicago: University of Chicago Press, 1976.

Chandler, Raymond. *Later Novels and Other Writings*. New York: Library of America, 1995.

Corner, John. *Critical Ideas in Television Studies*. Oxford: Clarendon, 1999.

109

Davidson, Jim. "Writing the Perry Mason Pilot: Interviews with TV Writers Ben Starr and Laurence Marks." *National Association for the Advancement of Perry Mason Newsletter*, no. 46 (winter 1990–91): 3–11.

Doyle, Aaron. "'Cops': Television Reality as Policing Reality." In *Entertaining Crime: Television Reality Programs*, ed. Mark Fishman and Gray Cavender, 95–116. New York: de Gruyter, 1998.

Dumble, Wende Vyborney. "And Justice for All: The Messages behind 'Real' Courtroom Dramas." In *Television Studies: Textual Analysis*, ed. Gary Burns and Robert J. Thompson, 103–18. New York: Praeger, 1989.

Dyer, Richard. *Only Entertainment*. London: Routledge, 1992.

Ellis, John. *Visible Fictions: Cinema: Television: Video*. Rev. ed. London: Routledge, 1992.

Fishman, Mark, and Gray Cavender, eds. *Entertaining Crime: Television Reality Programs*. New York: de Gruyter, 1998.

Fiske, John. *Television Culture*. London: Methuen, 1987.

Frank, Sam. *Buyer's Guide to 50 Years of TV on Video*. Amherst, NY: Prometheus, 1999.

Freud, Sigmund. *The Standard Edition of the Complete Psychological Works of Sigmund Freud*. Trans. and ed. James Strachey. 24 vols. London: Hogarth, 1959.

Gardner, Erle Stanley. *The Case of the Silent Partner*. 1940. Rpt. New York: Pocket Books, 1948.

———. *The Danger Zone and Other Stories*. Norfolk, VA: Crippen and Landru, 2004.

Geraghty, Christine, and David Lusted, eds. *The Television Studies Book*. London: Arnold, 1998.

Gerbner, George, and Larry Gross. "Living with Television: The Violence Profile." *Journal of Communication* 26 (1976): 173–99.

Graves, Robert, and Alan Hodge. *The Long Week End: A Social History of Great Britain, 1918–1939*. New York: Macmillan, 1941.

Habermas, Jürgen. *The Structural Transformation of the Public Sphere: An Inquiry into a Category of Bourgeois Society*. Trans. Thomas Burger, with the assistance of Frederick Lawrence. Cambridge: MIT Press, 1989.

Harris, Jay S., ed. *TV Guide: The First 25 Years*. New York: Simon and Schuster, 1978.

Hoover, Stewart M., Lynn Schofield Clark, and Diane F. Alters, with Joseph G. Champ and Lee Hood. *Media, Home, and Family*. New York: Routledge, 2004.

Hughes, Dorothy B., *Erle Stanley Gardner: The Case of the Real Perry Mason.* New York: Morrow, 1978.

Johnston, Alva. *The Case of Erle Stanley Gardner.* New York: Morrow, 1947.

Kelleher, Brian, and Diana Merrill. *The Perry Mason TV Show Book: The Complete Story of America's Favorite Television Lawyer, by Two of His Greatest Fans.* New York: St. Martin's, 1987.

Leonard, Elmore. "Writers on Writing: Easy on the Adverbs, Exclamation Points and Especially Hooptedoodle." *New York Times,* 16 July 2001, sec. E, p. 1.

Lewis, W. H. "Witness for the Prosecution." *TV Guide,* 30 November 1974, 5–7.

Marc, David, and Robert J. Thompson. *Prime Time, Prime Movers: From I Love Lucy to L.A. Law—America's Greatest TV Shows and the People Who Created Them.* Boston: Little, Brown, 1992.

Miller, Arthur. *Miller's Court.* Boston: Houghton Mifflin, 1982.

Post, Melville Davisson. *The Man of Last Resort: or, The Clients of Randolph Mason.* New York: Putnam, 1897.

Rapping, Elayne. *Law and Justice as Seen on TV.* New York: New York University Press, 2003.

Spigel, Lynn. *Make Room for TV: Television and the Family Ideal in Postwar America.* Chicago: University of Chicago Press, 1992.

———. "The Making of a TV Literate Elite." In *The Television Studies Book,* ed. Christine Geraghty and David Lusted, 63–85. London: Arnold, 1998.

"Sponsor Scope." *Sponsor,* 6 April 1957, 9.

Stark, Steven. "Perry Mason Meets Sonny Crockett: The History of Lawyers and the Police as Television Heroes." *University of Miami Law Review* 42 (1987): 229–83.

The Watergate and Related Activities. Phase I: Watergate Investigation. S Res. 60. Senate Select Committee on Presidential Campaign Activities, Presidential Campaign Activities of 1972. Book 3. 25 and 26 June 1973.

Watson, Colin. *Snobbery with Violence: Crime Stories and Their Audience.* London: Eyre and Spottiswoode, 1971.

Whitney, Dwight. "Pleading His Own Case." In *TV Guide: The First 25 Years,* ed. Jay S. Harris, 113–15. New York: Simon and Schuster, 1978.

Wober, Mallory, and Barrie Gunter. *Television and Social Control.* New York: St. Martin's, 1988.

Anatomy of a Murder. Directed by Otto Preminger. Screenplay by Wendell Mayes. Columbia. 1959.

. . . *And Justice for All*. Directed by Norman Jewison. Screenplay by Valerie Curtin and Barry Levinson. Columbia. 1979.

The Caine Mutiny. Directed by Edward Dmytryk. Screenplay by Stanley Roberts. Columbia. 1954.

"The Case of Constant Doyle." Directed by Allen H. Miner. Teleplay by Jackson Gillis. *Perry Mason*. CBS. 31 January 1963.

"The Case of Paul Drake's Dilemma." Directed by Jackson Gillis. Teleplay by Jackson Gillis, based on a story by Al C. Ward. *Perry Mason*. CBS. 14 November 1959. Columbia House Video Library, 1995.

"The Case of the Absent Artist." Directed by Arthur Marks. Teleplay by Robert C. Dennis. *Perry Mason*. CBS. 17 March 1962.

"The Case of the Angry Astronaut." Directed by Francis D. Lyon. Teleplay by Samuel Newman. *Perry Mason*. CBS. 7 April 1962. Columbia House Video Library, 1996.

"The Case of the Angry Dead Man." Directed by Arthur Marks. Teleplay by Michael Morris. *Perry Mason*. CBS. 25 February 1961.

"The Case of the Angry Mourner." Directed by William D. Russell. Teleplay by Francis Cockrill. *Perry Mason*. CBS. 2 November 1957. Columbia House Video Library, 1996.

"The Case of the Baited Hook." Directed by Christian Nyby. Teleplay by Richard Grey. *Perry Mason*. CBS. 21 December 1957. Columbia House Video Library, 1994.

"The Case of the Bashful Burro." Directed by Robert Ellis Miller. Teleplay by Jonathan Latimer. *Perry Mason*. CBS. 26 March 1960.

"The Case of the Bigamous Spouse." Directed by Arthur Marks. Teleplay by Jackson Gillis. *Perry Mason*. CBS. 14 November 1963. Columbia House Video Library, 2002.

The Case of the Black Cat. Directed by William McGann. Screenplay by F. Hugh Herbert. Warner Bros. 1936.

"The Case of the Black-Eyed Blonde." Directed by Roger Kay. Teleplay by Gene Wang. *Perry Mason*. CBS. 14 June 1958. Columbia House Video Library, 1995.

"The Case of the Blonde Bonanza." Directed by Arthur Marks. Teleplay by Jackson Gillis. *Perry Mason*. CBS. 17 December 1964. Columbia House Video Library, 2001.

"The Case of the Blushing Pearls." Directed by Richard B. Whorf. Teleplay by Jonathan Latimer. *Perry Mason*. CBS. 24 October 1959. Columbia House Video Library, 1994.

"The Case of the Bullied Bowler." Directed by Jesse Hibbs. Teleplay by Samuel Newman. *Perry Mason*. CBS. 5 November 1964.

"The Case of the Calendar Girl." Directed by Arthur Marks. Teleplay by Seeleg Lester. *Perry Mason*. CBS. 18 April 1959. Columbia House Video Library, 1994.

"The Case of the Carefree Coronary." Directed by Jesse Hibbs. Teleplay by Orville H. Hampton. *Perry Mason*. CBS. 17 October 1965. Columbia House Video Library, 1997.

"The Case of the Cowardly Lion." Directed by Arthur Marks. Teleplay by Jonathan Latimer. *Perry Mason*. CBS. 8 April 1961. Columbia House Video Library, 1996.

"The Case of the Crimson Kiss." Directed by Christian Nyby. Teleplay by Joel Murcott, Walter Doniger, and Milton Geiger. *Perry Mason*. CBS. 9 November 1957. Columbia House Video Library, 1997.

"The Case of the Crooked Candle." Directed by Christian Nyby. Teleplay by Robert Tallman. *Perry Mason*. CBS. 30 November 1957. Columbia House Video Library, 1994.

The Case of the Curious Bride. Directed by Michael Curtiz. Screenplay by Tom Reed. Warner Bros. 1935.

"The Case of the Dangerous Dowager." Directed by Buzz Kulik. Teleplay by Milton Krims. *Perry Mason*. CBS. 9 May 1959.

Columbia House Video Library, 1997.

"The Case of the Daring Decoy." Directed by Anton M. Leader. Teleplay by Seeleg Lester. *Perry Mason*. CBS. 29 March 1958. Columbia House Video Library, 1996.

"The Case of the Dead Ringer." Directed by Arthur Marks. Teleplay by Jackson Gillis. *Perry Mason*. CBS. 17 April 1966. Columbia House Video Library, 1997.

"The Case of the Deadly Verdict." Directed by Jesse Hibbs. Teleplay by Jonathan Latimer. *Perry Mason*. CBS. 3 October 1963. Columbia House Video Library, 2000.

"The Case of the Demure Defendant." Directed by Laslo Benedek. Teleplay by Ben Brady and Richard Grey. *Perry Mason*. CBS. 4 January 1958. Columbia House Video Library, 1995.

"The Case of the Drowning Duck." Directed by William D. Russell. Teleplay by Al C. Ward. *Perry Mason*. CBS. 12 October 1957. Columbia House Video Library, 1997.

"The Case of the Dubious Bridegroom." Directed by William D. Russell. Teleplay by Milton Krims. *Perry Mason*. CBS. 13 June 1959. Columbia House Video Library, 1997.

"The Case of the Fan-Dancer's Horse." Directed by William D. Russell. Teleplay by Sterling Silliphant. *Perry Mason*. CBS. 28 December 1957. Columbia House Video Library, 1998.

"The Case of the Final Fade-Out." Directed by Jesse Hibbs. Teleplay by Ernest Frankel and Orville H. Hampton. *Perry Mason*. CBS. 22 May 1966. Columbia House Video Library, 2001.

"The Case of the Fraudulent Photo." Directed by Arthur Marks. Teleplay by Lawrence J. Goldman and Seeleg Lester. *Perry Mason*. CBS. 7 February 1959. Columbia House Video Library, 1994.

"The Case of the Garrulous Gambler." Directed by Walter Grauman. Teleplay by Gene Wang. *Perry Mason*. CBS. 17 October 1959. Columbia House Video Library, 1997.

"The Case of the Gilded Lily." Directed by Andrew McLaglen. Teleplay by Richard Grey and Gene Wang. *Perry Mason*. CBS. 24 May 1958. Columbia House Video Library, 1995.

"The Case of the Glittering Goldfish." Directed by Gerd Oswald. Teleplay by Milton Krims and Gene Wang. *Perry Mason*. CBS. 17 January 1959. Columbia House Video Library, 1997.

"The Case of the Green-Eyed Sister." Directed by Christian Nyby. Teleplay by Richard Grey. *Perry Mason*. CBS. 8 February 1958. Columbia House Video Library, 1996.

"The Case of the Haunted Husband." Directed by Lewis Allen. Teleplay by Gene Wang. *Perry Mason*. CBS. 25 January 1958. Columbia House Video Library, 1997.

The Case of the Howling Dog. Directed by Alan Crosland. Screenplay by Ben Markson. Warner Bros. 1934.

"The Case of the Howling Dog." Directed by William D. Russell. Teleplay by Seeleg Lester. Teleplay by CBS. 11 April 1959. Columbia House Video Library, 1997.

"The Case of the Ice-Cold Hands." Directed by Jesse Hibbs. Teleplay by Jackson Gillis. *Perry Mason*. CBS. 23 January 1964. Columbia House Video Library, 1997.

"The Case of the Impatient Partner." Directed by Arthur Marks. Teleplay by Adrian Gendot. *Perry Mason*. CBS. 16 September 1961.

"The Case of the Jaded Joker." Directed by Gerd Oswald. Teleplay by Milton Krims and William L. Stuart. *Perry Mason*. CBS. 21 February 1959. Columbia House Video Library, 1996.

"The Case of the Jilted Jockey." Directed by William D. Russell. Teleplay by Robert Warnes Leach and Seeleg Lester. *Perry Mason*. CBS. 15 November 1958. Columbia House Video Library, 1997.

"The Case of the Lame Canary." Directed by Arthur Marks. Teleplay by Seeleg Lester. *Perry Mason*. CBS. 27 June 1959. Columbia House Video Library, 1998.

"The Case of the Lazy Lover." Directed by William D. Russell. Teleplay by Francis Cockrill. *Perry Mason*. CBS. 31 May 1958. Columbia House Video Library, 1996.

"The Case of the Left-Handed Liar." Directed by Jerry Hopper. Teleplay by Jonathan Latimer. *Perry Mason*. CBS. 25 November 1961.

"The Case of the Libelous Locket." Directed by Arthur Marks. Teleplay by Jonathan Latimer. *Perry Mason*. CBS. 7 February 1963.

"The Case of the Lonely Heiress." Directed by Laslo Benedek. Teleplay by Donald S. Sanford. *Perry Mason*. CBS. 1 February 1958. Columbia House Video Library, 1998.

"The Case of the Lost Last Act." Directed by Gerd Oswald. Teleplay by Milton Krims. *Perry Mason*. CBS. 21 March 1959. Columbia House Video Library, 1998.

The Case of the Lucky Legs. Directed by Archie Mayo. Screenplay by Ben Markson and Brown Holmes. Warner Bros. 1935.

"The Case of the Lucky Legs." Directed by Roger Kay. Teleplay by Maurice Zimm. *Perry Mason*. CBS. 19 December 1959. Columbia House Video Library, 1997.

"The Case of the Lucky Loser." Directed by William D. Russell. Teleplay by Seeleg Lester. *Perry Mason*. CBS. 27 September 1958. Columbia House Video Library, 1997.

"The Case of the Meddling Medium." Directed by Arthur Marks. Teleplay by Samuel Newman. *Perry Mason*. CBS. 21 October 1961. Columbia House Video Library, 1997.

"The Case of the Mischievous Doll." Directed by Jesse Hibbs. Teleplay by Jackson Gillis. *Perry Mason*. CBS. 13 May 1965.

"The Case of the Misguided Missile." Directed by John Peyser. Teleplay by Sol Stein and Glenn P. Wolfe. *Perry Mason*. CBS. 6 May 1961. Columbia House Video Library, 1997.

"The Case of the Moth-Eaten Mink." Directed by Ted Post. Teleplay by Laurence Marks and Ben Starr. *Perry Mason*. CBS. 14 December 1957. Columbia House Video Library, 1998.

"The Case of the Mystified Miner." Directed by Francis D. Lyon. Teleplay by Jackson Gillis. *Perry Mason*. CBS. 24 February 1962. Columbia House Video Library, 1996.

"The Case of the Mythical Monkeys." Directed by Gerald Thayer. Teleplay by Jonathan Latimer. *Perry Mason*. CBS. 27 February 1960. Columbia House Video Library, 1996.

"The Case of the Negligent Nymph." Directed by Christian Nyby. Teleplay by Richard Grey. *Perry Mason*. CBS. 7 December 1957. Columbia House Video Library, 1998.

"The Case of the Nervous Accomplice." Directed by William D. Russell. Teleplay by Sterling Silliphant. *Perry Mason*. CBS. 5 October 1957. Columbia House Video Library, 1995.

"The Case of the Prudent Prosecutor." Directed by Robert Ellis Miller. Teleplay by Jackson Gillis. *Perry Mason*. CBS. 30 January 1960. Columbia House Video Library, 1996.

"The Case of the Purple Woman." Directed by Gerd Oswald. Teleplay by Robert Bloomfield and Gene Wang. *Perry Mason*. CBS. 6 December 1958. Columbia House Video Library, 1995.

"The Case of the Restless Redhead." Directed by William D. Russell. Teleplay by Russell S. Hughes. *Perry Mason*. CBS. 21 September 1957. Columbia House Video Library, 1994.

"The Case of the Silent Partner." Directed by Christian Nyby. Teleplay by Donald S. Sanford. *Perry Mason*. CBS. 26 October 1957. Columbia House Video Library, 1994.

"The Case of the Singing Skirt." Directed by Arthur Marks. Teleplay by Jackson Gillis. *Perry Mason*. CBS. 12 March 1960. Columbia House

Video Library, 1996.

"The Case of the Slandered Submarine." Directed by Arthur Marks. Teleplay by Sam Newman. *Perry Mason*. CBS. 14 May 1960. Columbia House Video Library, 1997.

"The Case of the Spurious Sister." Directed by Arthur Marks. Teleplay by Maurice Zimm. *Perry Mason*. CBS. 3 October 1959. Columbia House Video Library, 2002.

The Case of the Stuttering Bishop. Directed by William Clemens. Screenplay by Don Ryan and Kenneth Gamet. Warner Bros. 1937.

"The Case of the Sulky Girl." Directed by Christian Nyby. Teleplay by Harold Swanton. *Perry Mason*. CBS. 19 October 1957. Columbia House Video Library, 1996.

"The Case of the Surplus Suitor." Directed by Jesse Hibbs. Teleplay by Robert C. Dennis. *Perry Mason*. CBS. 28 February 1963.

"The Case of the Terrified Typist." Directed by Andrew McLaglen. Teleplay by Robert C. Dennis, Philip Macdonald, and Ben Brady. *Perry Mason*. CBS. 21 June 1958. Columbia House Video Library, 1994.

"The Case of the Thermal Thief." Directed by Jack Arnold. Teleplay by Robert C. Dennis. *Perry Mason*. CBS. 14 January 1965.

"The Case of the Twice-Told Twist." Directed by Jesse Hibbs. Teleplay by Samuel Newman. *Perry Mason*. CBS. 27 February 1966. Columbia House Video Library, 1999.

"The Case of the Two-Faced Turnabout." Directed by Arthur Marks. Teleplay by Samuel Newman. *Perry Mason*. CBS. 14 February 1963.

"The Case of the Unwelcome Bride." Directed by Gilbert L. Kay. Teleplay by Helen Nielsen. *Perry Mason*. CBS. 16 December 1961. Columbia House Video Library, 1996.

The Case of the Velvet Claws. Directed by William Clemens. Screenplay by Tom Reed. Warner Bros. 1936.

"The Case of the Velvet Claws." Directed by Harmon Jones. Teleplay by Jackson Gillis. *Perry Mason*. CBS. 21 March 1963. Columbia House Video Library, 1998.

Counsellor at Law. Directed by William Wyler. Screenplay by Elmer Rice. Universal. 1933.

Erin Brockovich. Directed by Steven Soderburgh. Screenplay by Susannah Grant. Jersey/Universal. 2000.

A Few Good Men. Directed by Rob Reiner. Screenplay by Aaron Sorkin. Columbia TriStar. 1992.

The Firm. Directed by Sydney Pollack. Screenplay by David Rabe. Paramount. 1993.

Fury. Directed by Fritz Lang. Screenplay by Bartlett Cormack and Fritz Lang. MGM. 1936.

Gentlemen Prefer Blondes. Directed by Howard Hawks. Screenplay by Charles Lederer. 20th Century–Fox. 1953.

Granny Get Your Gun. Directed by George Amy. Screenplay by Kenneth Gamet. Warner Bros. 1939.

I Confess. Directed by Alfred Hitchcock. Screenplay by George Tabori and William Archibald. Warner Bros. 1952.

Inherit the Wind. Directed by Stanley Kramer. Screenplay by Nathan E. Douglas and Harold Jacob Smith. United Artists. 1960.

"Marty." Directed by Delbert Mann. Teleplay by Paddy Chayefsky. *Goodyear Television Playhouse.* NBC. 1953.

Miracle on 34th Street. Written and directed by George Seaton. 20th Century–Fox. 1947.

The Paradine Case. Directed by Alfred Hitchcock. Screenplay by David O. Selznick. Selznick International, 1947.

"*Perry Mason* Returns." Directed by Ron Satlof. Teleplay by Dean Hargrove. NBC. 1 December 1985.

"*Perry Mason*: The Case of the All-Star Assassin." Directed by Christian I. Nyby II. Teleplay by Dean Hargrove, Joel Steiger, and Robert Hamilton. NBC. 19 November 1989.

"*Perry Mason*: The Case of the Killer Kiss." Directed by Christian I. Nyby II. Teleplay by Gerry Conway. NBC. 29 November 1993.

"*Perry Mason*: The Case of the Lost Love." Directed by Ron Satlof. Teleplay by Anne Collins. NBC. 23 February 1987.

"*Perry Mason*: The Case of the Maligned Monster." Directed by Ron Satlof. Teleplay by Sean Cholodenko. NBC. 11 February 1991.

"*Perry Mason*: The Case of the Notorious Nun." Directed by Ron Satlof. Teleplay by Joel Steiger. NBC. 25 May 1986.

"*Perry Mason*: The Case of the Shooting Star." Directed by Ron Satlof. Teleplay by Anne Collins and Dean Hargrove. NBC. 9 November 1986.

"*Perry Mason*: The Case of the Skin-Deep Scandal." Directed by Christian I. Nyby II. Teleplay by Robert Schlitt. NBC. 19 February 1993.

Presumed Innocent. Directed by Alan J. Pakula. Screenplay by Frank Pierson and Alan J. Pakula. Warner Bros. 1990.

"Requiem for a Heavyweight." Directed by Ralph Nelson and Alvin Rakoff. Teleplay by Rod Serling. *Playhouse 90*. CBS. 1956.

Sergeant Rutledge. Directed by John Ford. Screenplay by James Warner Bellah and Willis Goldbeck. Warner Bros. 1960.

To Kill a Mockingbird. Directed by Alan J. Pakula. Screenplay by Horton Foote. Universal-International. 1962.

The Verdict. Directed by Sidney Lumet. Screenplay by David Mamet. 20th Century–Fox. 1982.

Witness for the Prosecution. Directed by Billy Wilder. Screenplay by Billy Wilder and Harry Kurnitz. United Artists. 1957.

When books, films, comics, and radio and television programs bear the same titles, they are listed separately and chronologically. Otherwise unidentified entries in quotation marks refer to television episodes. Fictional characters are indexed only if they appear in more than a single work. Titles of books and essays are indexed only when they are mentioned in the text, and names in the notes are indexed only when there is no direct reference to them in the corresponding passage in the text. Page numbers in bold refer to illustrations.

129